A – Z Football/Soccer Coaching

ADRIAN WEBSTER

Copyright © 2020 Adrian Webster

A-Z Football/Soccer Coaching

Books to Go Now

All rights reserved

Excerpt from A – Z Football/Soccer Coaching

I want my team to be a forward – thinking team that asks questions of the opposition.

Control, Pass and Move will be the foundation of our team strategy, however players will also be encouraged to express themselves in the right areas.

As I have already said, the game is not rocket science and in simple terms is made up of defending and attacking principles. Defending starts as soon as you lose possession and attacking as soon as you regain possession. Players must understand they have a part to play in both defending and attacking.

Drawing of Adrian Webster by John Best

Table of Contents

Dedication	7
Introduction	8
Adrian Webster Career	10
Alphabet Football	12
My Team	14
How I want my team to play	23
Control, Pass and Move	26
Understanding of Individual roles	31
Team Shape and Balance	42
Principles of Football/Soccer	49
Systems	55
Patterns of play	57
8 v 8	61
Set pieces	63
Components of Football/Soccer	71
Tactics	79
Physical Fitness	81
Psychology – Mental Alertness	87
Principles of Coaching	89
The Coach – Player Relationship	91
Organisation	96

Pre – Season	98
Role Models	110
My Football/Soccer Philosophy	114
Summary	115
Fantasy Football	120
A Guide to Soccer and Coaching Ade's Way	121
Circle of Life: A Life, A Career, A Passion from Former Seattle Sounders Team Captain	122
Adrian Webster	123
Books to Go Now	124

Dedication

I would like to dedicate this book to Alan Hudson who was the person most responsible for getting me to put pen to paper. Also to Jenni Conner at Books to Go Now who has kindly published all eight books and to everyone who has purchased a copy in support of Children with Cancer to whom I donate all my proceeds. A Big Thank You!

Introduction

Initially I wrote about my football/soccer journey which spans a little over 50 years. More recently I have written two coaching books based on my football/soccer experiences and how I would like my team to play.

When I left school in 1968 to join my home town club Colchester United my ambition was to become a professional footballer and to play for the first team. For those of you that have read my book Circle of Life you will see that it didn't quite go to plan.

In 1974 I signed for the Seattle Sounders a new franchise in the NASL (North American Soccer League). During my six seasons of playing for them I was encouraged by Head Coach John Best and his assistant Jimmy Gabriel to think about coaching after my playing days. Through getting involved in the Sounders off season coaching program it got me thinking more about my own game and with the help of John and Jimmy I think my game improved tremendously.

In the 79 – 80 season while playing for the Phoenix Inferno in the MISL (Major Indoor Soccer League) I sustained an injury and was asked to take over the role of coach. We went onto win 11 out of the last 13 games and made it into the playoffs. The following season I was made Head Coach and this was the beginning of my coaching career.

During my coaching career I have coached youth, college and pro's, working with senior players as well as with the Arizona State and the Region IV Women's teams.

Before returning to England in November 1991 a few days before my 40th birthday I went up to Seattle to do my USSF 'B' Licence. Although I didn't have a job to go back to I felt that I had a much better chance of staying in the game in England as the game in the US was going through a transition period and I hoped my 10 years of coaching plus my coaching qualifications would open a few doors.

Although I had been away almost 20 years I still had friends and contacts that were involved in the game and by late November I became Manager of Brightlingsea United FC in the Jewson Premier League. I went onto coach and manage for 25 years before retiring just before my 65th birthday.

ADRIAN WEBSTER CAREER

Playing career

1968 – 1982   Colchester United England
Hillingdon Borough England
Vancouver Spartans Canada
Seattle Sounders USA
Pittsburgh Spirit USA.
Phoenix Inferno USA

Coaching career

1982-1987   Phoenix Inferno
Phoenix Sports Centre
Scottsdale Community College

1988 – 1990	Arizona Condors – GM/Head Coach
1991 – 1992	Brightlingsea United FC – Manager
1992 – 1993	Halstead Town FC – Manager
1993 – 2006	Colchester United FC Summer Camp Coordinator Soccer Centre Manager C of E U16 Coach Recruitment Officer YDO/C of E Manager U9 – U16
2006 – 2016	Colne Community College Assistant Director of Football

Alphabet Football

Before I continue I would like you to do as I have done below an A – Z one word that is relevant to football/soccer.

- **A.** Awareness
- **B.** Balance
- **C.** Composure
- **D.** Discipline
- **E.** Endurance
- **F.** Flexibility
- **G.** Goals
- **H.** Heading
- **I.** Impact
- **J.** Jockey
- **K.** Knowledge
- **L.** Leader
- **M.** Movement
- **N.** Nutrition
- **O.** Organisation
- **P.** Passing
- **Q.** Quick
- **R.** Reliable
- **S.** Speed
- **T.** Touch
- **U.** Understanding

V. Vision
W. Winner
X. X- Factor
Y. Yearning
Z. Zone

As a coach when I watch a game l look at it very much like I did when I was a player, looking at what we did well and the areas we need to improve on. As a Coach/Manager you are responsible for getting the best out of your players/team in performing to the best of their ability. Over the years there have been many changes within the game and coaches now have to think more about how they pre – pare their team ie number of games a week, training methods, diet and rest.

When I first took over coaching a team the first thing I looked at was to change the system. Now as a coach I find myself talking more about team shape and balance and building my team around what the players strengths and weaknesses are. For me systems of play are the foundation for defending and attacking principles and players need to be able to make the transition when losing or regaining possession of the ball.

My Team

Football/Soccer is a team sport and ideally my team would consist of players that are coachable, able to take on board the information they are given and apply it in both training and games. Training is about developing good habits and prepares you for your match play.

The type of player I am looking for should be enthusiastic and have a positive attitude to both training and playing.

As the coach, it is my responsibility to create a healthy and learning working environment, whereby players are encouraged to express themselves without fear of making mistakes.

Being comfortable with the ball is very important to how I want my team to play and at sixteen years old, I feel players should be technically sound.

Football/Soccer is not rocket science and for players to improve their game, they need to work with the ball. Being able to use both feet will afford you a bit more time and space.

The game is made up of defending and attacking principles and I want my players to be able to make the transition when losing or regaining possession of the ball. Therefore, players need to have a good understanding of the principles required in both defending and attacking.

During my playing and coaching days I played in various systems and organised my teams to play a certain system. If I was coaching today I think my preferred system would be 3 – 5 – 2 see Diagram 1.

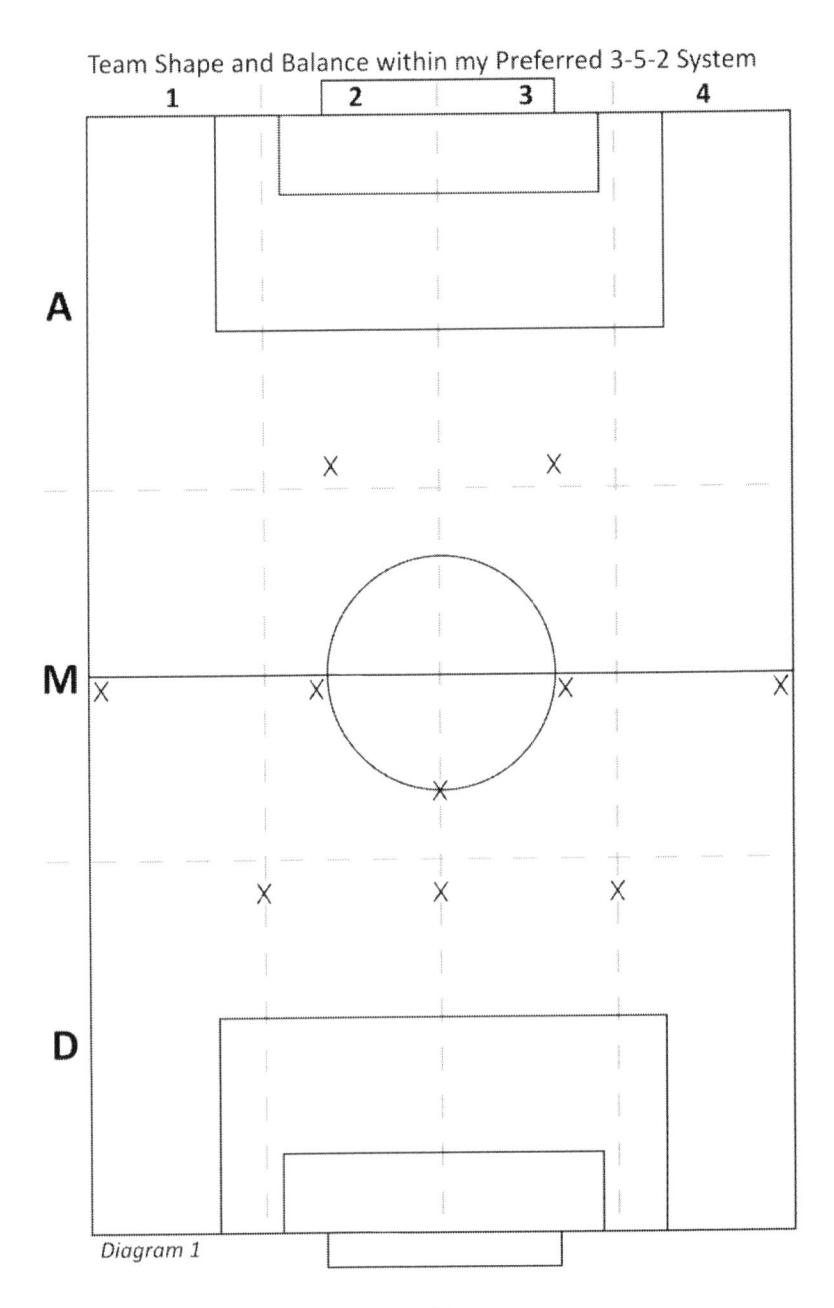

Team Shape and Balance within my Preferred 3-5-2 System

| 1 | 2 | 3 | 4 |

A

M

D

Diagram 1

I would want my three CBs to defend the width of the penalty box and not to sit to deep. The role of my GK is Keeper/Sweeper, he would need to be a good communicator and comfortable with the ball at his feet. In midfield, I would have a holding player (to screen the back three) who must also be a good communicator and disciplined in his role. Either side of my holding player I want an attacking midfielder that has 10 – 15 goals in him and a creative midfielder who is able to spray the ball around.

Outside of the three CM players, I want two wide players that work from box to box and are able to deliver good crosses into the penalty area. Depending on which one is delivering the cross, I want the one on the other side to look at getting into the box by timing his run and to be a far post threat.

I want my two front players to engage the CBs and look to move them around. I would prefer they stayed out of the wide channels and look to get into the box at every opportunity.

I also think that it is important to have a strong bench and I want players that can come on and have an impact.

Practice makes permanent and that is why I like to work with 16 players, I just feel that you can accomplish so much more in your sessions by creating the right working environment.

I also think it is important to have a backup plan, sometimes when you play with two up front and the opposition are playing a flat back four it is difficult to stop the opposition's FBs from getting out. In this situation I would think about taking off my holding midfielder and to push another player up front going to a 3 – 4 – 3.

Playing 3 – 4 – 3 creates 3 diamonds across the pitch and gives you good width and depth. (shape and balance). See diagram 2.

From an attacking point of view the first thing I would ask of my 3 front players, is to push right up on their back four as illustrated:

X   O   X   O   X   O   X

By playing in – between the defenders this asks questions straightaway of *who is marking who?*

Defensively I would get the 3 forwards to drop off to encourage the opposition to play out from the back and then look to press quickly ie.

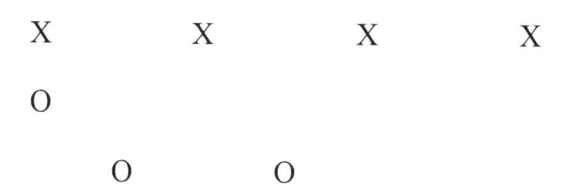

```
    X         X         X         X
    O
         O         O
```

This does two things defensively 1. Keeps the play in front of us and 2. Affords our midfield and defenders time to provide good shape and balance.

Looking at the 3 – 4 – 3 system, where I think the team might be a little vulnerable, is if the opposition play with three central midfielders and if they play balls into the wide channels in our defensive third. In that situation I would revert to 3 – 5 – 2 which would balance the overload in the centre of midfield and I would emphasise the importance of the three CBs slotting over and for the two wide players to track back.

Players are required to perform to the best of their ability for a period of up to ninety minutes, therefore it is very important that the team has a good fitness base. I want my team to play at a high tempo, but also to be able to slow it down and keep possession when needed.

Players need to know how their body works and the importance of a healthy diet, as well as rest to help their recovery so they are able to do it all over again. For me, fitness is the foundation to putting together an entertaining and winning team.

When coaching kids, the coach should not lose sight that it is a development program. For players 16 – 19 years old, we are preparing them to make the step up to senior football and I believe they have to earn the right to start. I don't think there is anything wrong in developing a winning mentality.

For every winning team, there has to be a losing team, therefore my emphasis will be on trying to get the performance right because I believe that if you do so more often than not, the result will go hand in glove. Sometimes, you will be the better team and still not get the result, which I can accept if I feel we have given it our best effort and tried to do it the right way.

Once we have established a good fitness base, I will put forward to the team how I would like them to play, making sure they understand clearly our strategy. It is important that I keep an open mind and allow the players to have an input, as I want them to believe and sign up to what our goals are for the season.

When putting your team together, I think before establishing what system or how you want to play, you have to take a look at the strengths and weaknesses of the players you are working with. I also like to balance my team out with a few natural left – sided players.

3 Diamonds Width and Depth within a 3-4-3 System

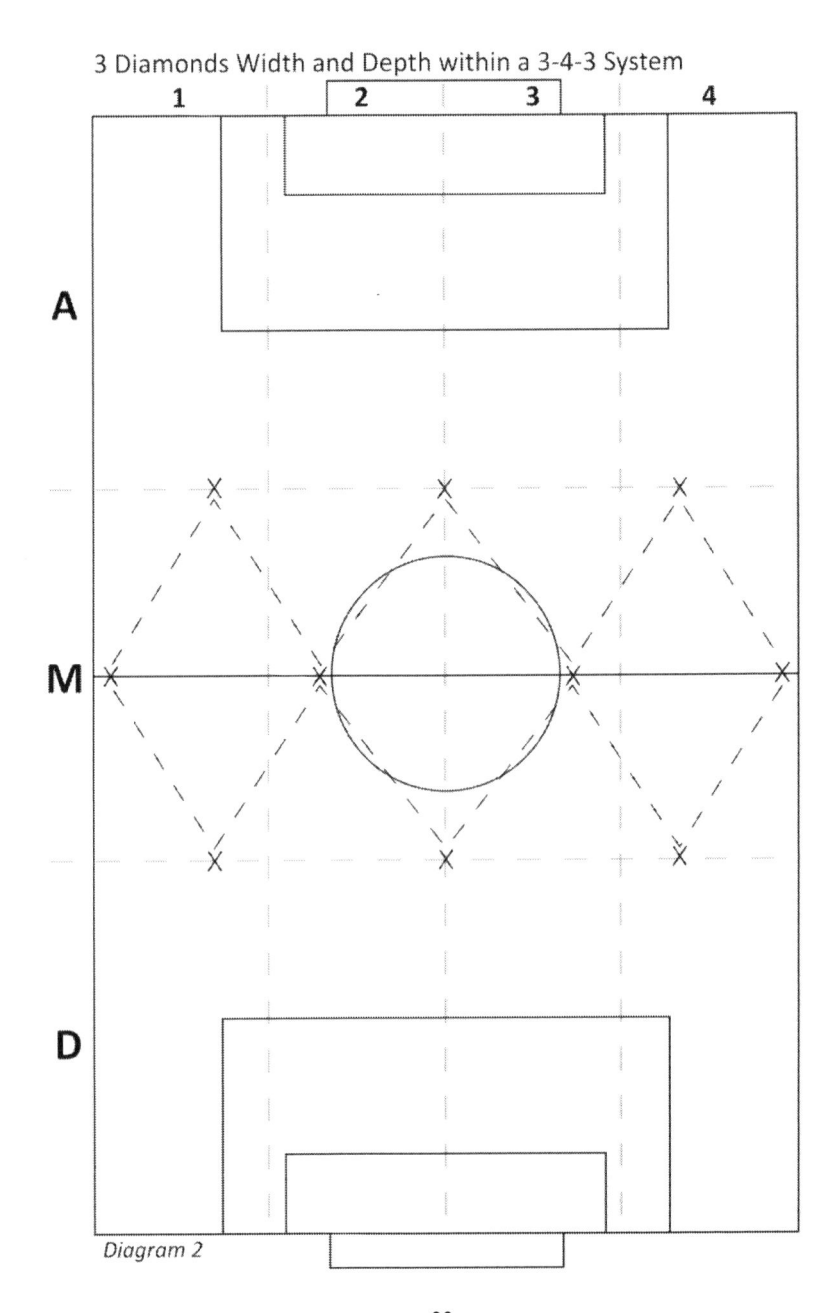

Diagram 2

How I want my team to play

I want my team to be a forward – thinking team that asks questions of the opposition.

Control, Pass and Move will be the foundation of our team strategy, however players will also be encouraged to express themselves in the right areas.

As I have already mentioned, the game is not rocket science and in simple terms is made up of defending and attacking principles. Defending starts as soon as you lose possession and attacking as soon as you regain possession. Players must understand they have a part to play in both defending and attacking.

In the game you are under pressure in 3 ways: your opponent, space and time. The better players are the ones that make the right decisions more often.

Goals and clean sheets win games. Good possession gives you a better chance. Good preparation is therefore the key to giving your team the best possible chance.

I would like for my team to try to play out from the back when it is on to do so. Trusting your teammates and an understanding of your role, is important in good build – up play.   An early picture and a good first touch will help your decision – making.

At some point in the game, regardless of your position, you will be under pressure and I think every player should have in their repertoire a move or two to get themselves out of trouble. When receiving the ball, try not to panic, think ' *control and manoeuvre.* ' Doing so, will afford you a bit more time and space. If your first touch is forward, be positive and look to pass or run the ball forward. Remember, the ball will never get tired and it can travel quicker than you, so make the ball do the work.

Within our team structure, I like to work on patterns of play, so players can get a better understanding of good support.

When being marked, make your first movement away from the ball and when checking back to receive it, try to be sideways on. This way, you can see where the ball is coming from and where you want to go with it.

After having surgery on my back in October 2019, and in- between doing my rehab, I found myself watching a lot of Premier League games (before the Coronavirus Pandemic) and to be quite honest, I found them to be a bit boring. What I mean by that is, a lot of the teams are trying to adapt the Man. City style of play (playing out from the back), and in my opinion, they are not good enough. For me, there are too many backward and square passes that are being intercepted and teams are getting punished. On paper, Wolves and Sheffield United don't have the strength and quality of some of the top teams, however what they have brought to the league is a good work ethic and a bit more directness in their play. This got me to thinking about what these teams are doing in training and how has the modern day method of coaching changed the game.

When I was a player, I was taught that when receiving the ball, to have an early picture, get the ball out from under your feet and look to play it forward. By doing so, you straight away ask questions of the opposition.

I don't want to be seen as advocating the long ball game, because for me it is more about getting the balance right and again good team shape and balance and angles and distance of support is relevant to good buildup play.

Control, Pass and Move

Control. There are two ways of bringing the ball under control. They are *Cushion control and Wedge Control.* When bringing the ball under control think Control and Manoeuvre. This affords you a bit more time and space. Cushion control is taking the pace off of the ball using your foot, thigh, chest or head by relaxing on contact with the ball. With Wedge control it is about getting your body behind the ball and placing the body surface over the ball to stop it bouncing back up at you. When having the ball under control you have two options, you can either run with it or pass it.

Pass. An early picture and a good first touch helps your decision making. You don't have to be a George Best and be able to dribble the ball around half a dozen players. You can accomplish that with one well executed pass of the ball. When making a pass, coaches will talk about pass consideration – accuracy and the pace of the pass. If you are not accurate, but the pace or the weight of the pass is right, the player looking to receive it can always get to it. An early picture will help determine whether you play the ball into his feet or into the space. Distance will determine the type of pass and you have three options.

1. *Push pass* using the inside of the foot over a shorter distance.
2. *Driven pass* using the lace area of the boot – played more firmly to prevent interception.
3. With the *Lofted pass,* you use the big toe area of your foot looking to play the ball to a teammate through the air. With the *Chip pass,* there is no follow through. This gets the ball up quickly over the midfield area and because it is clipped, it puts back spin on the ball and it fades into the path of the receiver.

When making a pass, make your first look forward and when trying to penetrate the oppositions defence, play it with a bit more pace so not to get intercepted.

Good control and passing equals good possession.

Move. Movement asks questions of the opposition. We encourage players to move after making a pass to do two things.

1. To give his teammate the option of playing the ball back to him, or
2. To play the ball into the space he has created for another teammate to come into that space. It doesn't have to be a thirty yard run but by just changing the angle gives your teammate another option.

Good passing and movement (combination play) in and around the penalty area makes it difficult to defend against. When receiving the ball and laying it off, make your first movement away from the ball. This asks questions of the defender who now has to make a decision whether to stay with you or to defend the space. When looking to exploit the space a change of pace makes it even more difficult for the defender.

A-Z FOOTBALL/SOCCER COACHING

Passing and Moving Drills

1.

Follow your pass

X^1 passes to X^2, X^2 to X^3 etc.

X^1 takes the position of X^2,

X^2 takes position of X^3 etc.

Opposite Direction

2.

X^1 and X^2 Pass to X^3 and X^4

X^3 and X^4 Play the ball back and crossover

Switch over

Variaton:

This exercise can be served from hands for Volley/Header return

Key:

O - Ball

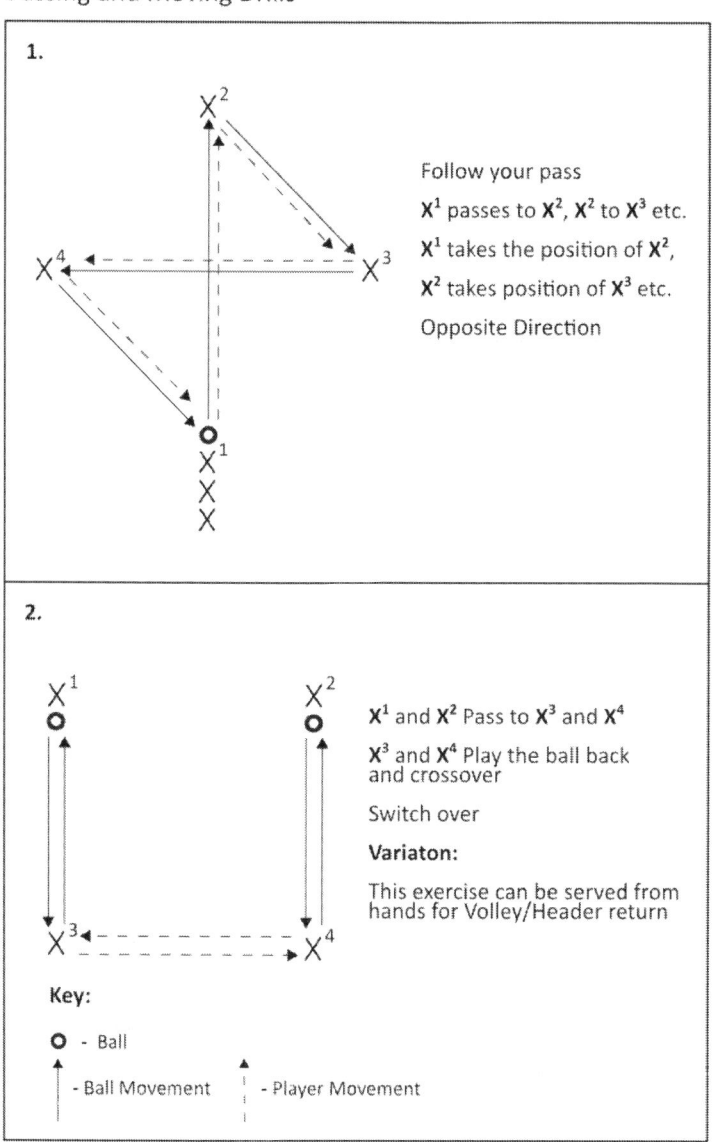

- Ball Movement

- Player Movement

Diagram3a

Passing and Moving Drills

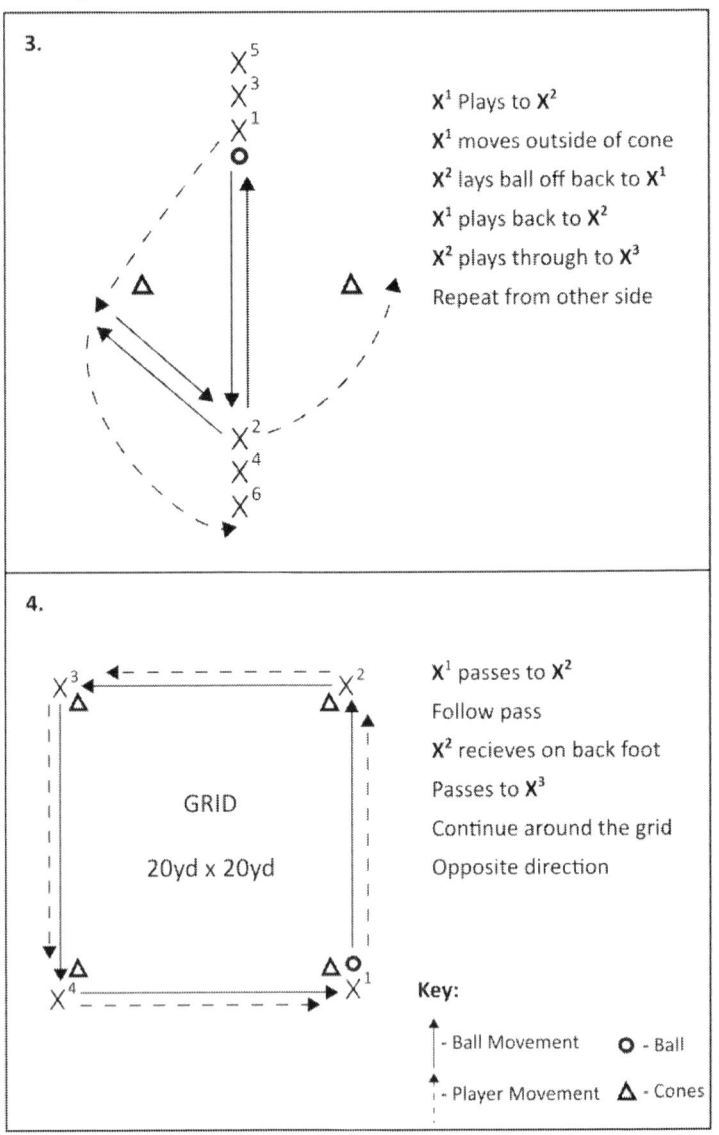

3.

X^1 Plays to X^2

X^1 moves outside of cone

X^2 lays ball off back to X^1

X^1 plays back to X^2

X^2 plays through to X^3

Repeat from other side

4.

GRID

20yd x 20yd

X^1 passes to X^2

Follow pass

X^2 recieves on back foot

Passes to X^3

Continue around the grid

Opposite direction

Key:

↑ - Ball Movement   O - Ball

↑ - Player Movement   △ - Cones

Diagram 3b

Understanding of Individual roles

Having coached 10 years at the Colne Football College in Brightlingsea we often picked up young players that had been involved at pro clubs Academies and I found it a bit frustrating of their lack of understanding of their role within the team. It is all very well saying we are going to play a 4 – 4 – 2, 4 – 3 – 3 or a 3 – 4 – 3 and expect young players to adapt without working on it and for me this is where good team shape and balance comes into play. There are several formations available to football/soccer strategists, but at the basic level, this includes the following broad positions GK (Goal Keeper) , Defenders, Midfielders and Forwards.

Whilst those familiar with football/soccer should already be aware of this, for anyone **new** to the game – such as a coach transitioning to football/soccer from another sport, or for a novice player just beginning to learn – this knowledge might not be so obvious. For the sake of clarity, this is how the positions mentioned above can typically align in a traditional 4 – 4 – 2 formation, although there are many variations to this line – up depending on tactical choices which I will explain later in the book.

GOALKEEPER

| RIGHT BACK | CENTRE BACK | CENTRE BACK | LEFT BACK |

| RIGHT WING | CENTRE MID | CENTRE MID | LEFT WING |

FORWARD   FORWARD

Now let's look at each position in a bit more depth:

Gk. The primary job of the GK is to stop the ball going into the back of the net. However, I want my GK to play a more important role and to be the Keeper/Sweeper. Therefore I would expect him to be comfortable with the ball at his feet.

Most keepers I have played with have been good shot stoppers and there main weakness has been dealing with crosses. I want my keeper to have good agility and to be brave when dealing with crosses, read the flight of the ball, leave it late and come quickly. Good lateral movement is important, do not cross your feet over. When in possession of the ball, get to the edge of your box quickly, looking to setup a quick counterattack.

Good communication is important, don't allow your defenders to drop too deep. As well as being the last line of defence, he can also be the the start of an attack, therefore a good starting position is essential. A good first touch and being able to use both feet, is also a bonus!

Defenders. FB (Right and Left Back). I want my FB's to be able to play from box to box. Therefore, they need to have a good understanding of defending and attacking principles, as well as have good speed endurance.

When I first started to play FB , I was encouraged to take up a wide position when the keeper had the ball and told to get the ball into the front player's and to push up quickly.

When I went to play for the Seattle Sounders, both coaches Best and Gabriel, talked about and showed me the importance of the quality of service into the front player's. I had the habit of trying to hit the inch perfect pass and it was Jimmy Gabriel who told me to just try to drop the ball into the space in front of the receiver for him to come onto it. He showed me how to get the ball up quickly over the midfield and how to put backspin on the ball so it would fade into the space in front of my target.

In my first couple of seasons of playing FB, I was told to support the wide player playing in front of me from behind so that if he was unable to get his cross in, I was available for him to roll the ball back for me to play it into the penalty area from a slightly deeper position.

Another thing we worked on was the timing of the overlap and the delivery of the ball into the attacking third where the emphasis was on missing out the first defender with your cross.

In today's modern game FBs or Wing Backs as they are now called are more evident than the good old – fashioned wingers who made a living out of taking on the FB and getting his cross in. I also remember early on when going on a overlap and trying to get my cross in many of them going behind the goal and again it was Jimmy Gabriel telling me to make my last touch before crossing it slightly inside as well as showing me how to deliver the ball Beckham – like (not quite as effective as Beckham), by hitting across the ball which bends the ball away from the keeper and defenders into the path of the attacking players.

As a FB, you are often up against quick players, so good pace is important. Not only are you expected to get forward when the ball is on your side of the field, you are also responsible for providing cover for your CBs when the opposition are attacking down the other side of the field. Your body shape and movement of the head enables you to see both the ball and your opponent. A lot of crosses delivered into the penalty area are hit deep, so the FB needs to be a good header of the ball.

CB. Centre Back. The qualities I look for in a good CB are pace/mobility, a good range of passing and good in the air. Playing CB quite often means you are matched up against the oppositions key player who is either mobile and scores goals or is a big strong target man and usually an aerial threat. The key to good defending is to stop your opponent from turning, stay on your feet and don't dive in. By marking goal side and ball side, you stand less chance of getting boxed in and you might be able to step in front of your opponent to intercept the ball. Good use of the ball is very important in playing out from the back and a good range of passing is key to trying to exploit the opposition's defensive setup. Obviously height can be an advantage when challenging for the ball in the air, but the timing of your jump and good spring is key to winning the ball and all CBs should work on this regularly in training.

Midfield. (Wing play). In today's modern game wing play can be a combination of the FB and Winger or just the Wingback. Either way it is important that the players involved have a good understanding of defending and attacking principles. The primary job of the wide player in going forward is to is to provide crosses into the penalty area and defensively to track back when losing possession of the ball.

As a Wingback speed endurance is essential in or out of possession of the ball and I can remember Harry Redknapp saying to our wide players when you receive the ball go quickly at the defender, look to attack his front foot (the best he can do is to try to flick the ball away). If you go outside think cross if you go inside think shot.

When the ball is being played to the wide player the opposition's defender is looking to close him down quickly to stop him from getting a run at him. In this situation the wide player needs to have a move or two up his sleeve. The best example I can give of a player creating a yard or two of space for himself and delivering the inch perfect cross is David Beckham, very seldom did you see him go by the defender.

When the ball is on the opposite side of the pitch make your recovery run towards the corner of the 18 yard box. By doing so you are providing cover for your CBs, however you also need to be aware of the wide player on your side so keep moving your head and in your set position have an open body so you can see both the ball and the player trying to get in around the back.

When defending in your defensive third and your keeper regains possession of the ball, I want my two wide players to try to hit the halfway line as quickly as possible. This does two things:

1. We maybe able to hit the opposition on the counter attack if there players are lazy in reacting, or
2. By doing so, we also create space for our CBs to split and for us to look to play out from the back.

CM. (Central Midfielders). During the 1977 season Head Coach Jimmy Gabriel moved me into a holding midfield role where my job was to screen the back four, win my tackles and to give it to the more creative players. It was a bonus that I was able to use both feet, had a good range of passing and was decent in the air.

As a three in midfield, we had a nice balance of an attacking midfielder, a holding midfielder and a creative midfielder (Jenkins, Webster and Buttle). We would use the centre circle as a guide to help keep our shape and balance as well as create good angles and distance of support. As the holding midfielder (and because I played behind the other two) communication was very important and as a unit we tried to keep the play in front of us.

Tommy Jenkins was very good at running at the opposition and committing them by playing into and off of our front players, whereas Steve Buttle was very good at finding little pockets of space. He was very comfortable with the ball, and very seldom gave it away. His decision making was very good and he was excellent at hitting those penetrating passes.

Midfield is the link between the defenders and forwards and angles and distance of support is very important. When receiving the ball, try to get sideways on and take it on your back foot this way you can see where it is coming from and where you want to go with it. An early picture and a good first touch helps your decision making and when ever possible try to run or pass the ball forward. I once worked with a coach who use to drill it into his players continuously to pass the ball square and back to keep possession so much it made the opposition's job of defending so much easier. I would say to him if that's the way you want your team to play then you should move the goals to the side of the pitch. My point being it is those penetrating passes and forward runs with the ball that ask questions of the opposition. In the final third you have to be brave and prepared to take chances!

Today if I was putting my midfield unit together I

would be looking for a player who is going to kick in with 10 – 15 goals a season (a Steve Gerrard or a Frank Lampard). The midfield is often referred to as the 'engine room' and players like Gerrard and Lampard covered a lot of ground, therefore it is essential to have a good fitness base. I think the key to having a rounded midfield is discipline and an understanding of your role.

FWDS. (Forwards). I personally don't like to play with just one up top, but much prefer a partnership or a unit of three. No matter how we setup, I want my front players to be mobile because movement causes problems for defenders. Obviously, certain players bring different qualities to the table and it is all about how the coach utilises each player's strengths. Whether we play with two or three up front I want one of those players to be a good target man, someone we can play the ball into and off of as well as hold it up in tight situations and to also be an aerial threat.

The primary job of our front players is to create and score goals, however I want my front player's to realise that they also have defensive responsibilities. When the opposition's GK has the ball, if working as a partnership I want them to drop off together, thereby encouraging the opposition to play out from the back. When the ball is rolled out to one of the defenders, I want the nearest front player to look to apply pressure by looping his run and to show him inside, the other forward would then drop off to stop the forward pass.

This would do two things for us:

1. Keep the play in front of us.
2. Afford our midfield and defenders time to take up good defending shape and balance.

If my front player's apply there defensive responsibilities I am not particularly bothered about them chasing all the way back into our defensive third of the pitch, because we should still have enough bodies back. If we leave two players up, they will probably leave 3 back plus the GK, so we will still have a numerical advantage of 9 v 7. By applying this strategy we can give our front player's a little bit more recovery time allowing them to be more dynamic in and around the opposition's penalty box.

In the attacking third, I want my players to take chances and the one thing I always say to them is, ' The goal never moves ' I try to encourage them to get sideways on when receiving the ball so they can protect it better, see where it is coming from and where they want to go with it. When getting shots and headers off, it is important to work the keeper and to follow in for rebounds!

Another thing I am not really keen on is my front player's making runs into the wide channels. I tell them to leave the channels open for the wide players and to just concentrate on getting into the box.

ADRIAN WEBSTER

Team Shape and Balance

The mechanics of team shape is like breathing in and out

Breathing in and (expanding) to provide width and create our attacking shape.

Breathing out and (contracting) to get our defensive shape – compactness and balance.

Good team shape requires:

1. Good support – linking the defence, midfield and forwards.
2. Angles and distance between players.
3. An understanding of how offside is dealt with collectively.
4. Utilisation of width – in attacking mode or compactness defensively.

From a strategy perspective in keeping good team shape and balance, think in terms of thirds of the pitch.

Attacking third: Positive attitude, take risks.

Middle third: Build – up zone, keeping possession. Decision – making when to play forward.

Defending third: The no – nonsense zone. Safety first.

Possession of the ball is very important, but it does not necessarily win you games. Goals and clean sheets win games!

When I first came back from America, I went to watch my nephew play. He played CM and on the ball, he looked a very good player. However, like many young players, he didn't really have a good understanding of his role and wanted to be everywhere the ball was. Consequently, when he got into the final third where he needed that bit of quality, he was to tired to have an impact. After the game I was approached by his coach and he asked my opinion. The first thing I asked him was what system were they playing and he said it was suppose to be 4 – 4 – 2 and we both agreed it looked a bit disjointed. He then asked me if I would do a session on the board with them and then take it out onto the pitch.

Diagram 4 - Team Shape and Balance within a 4 – 4 – 2 system:

The first thing I showed them was how I try to make it easy for my players to maintain good shape and balance. Firstly I divided the pitch into thirds, defending, midfield and attack, I then added four channels and then laid out there 4 – 4 – 2 system asking them to take a look at the position they played. I then proceeded to talk about the importance of good team shape and balance in and out of possession of the ball. I reminded them that we only play with one ball and what we want to try to do is to provide good support by playing as a team through the thirds of the pitch up and down the channel relevant to their position.

Diagram 5 - Defending Shape and Balance within a 4 – 4 – 2 system:

Defensively, 4 – 4 – 2 gives you two banks of four with the GK playing a keeper/sweeper role. The back four are nice and compact and not to deep. The dotted lines from the halfway line back to the corner of the penalty area are a guide for FBs and Wingers tracking back. If the opposition are attacking through the middle, the two forwards will normally drop back to the halfway line. If attacking down one side, the forwards will slot over.

Diagram 6 - Attacking Shape and Balance within a 4 – 4 – 2 system:

Offensively, we are looking to stretch the opposition. Therefore, good width and depth (angles and distance of support) is the key. When the RB is on the ball the two forwards slot over so he now has a first and second striker he can play into. The nearest CM and Winger provide support either side creating a diamond shape and the other players provide good shape and balance.

A-Z FOOTBALL/SOCCER COACHING

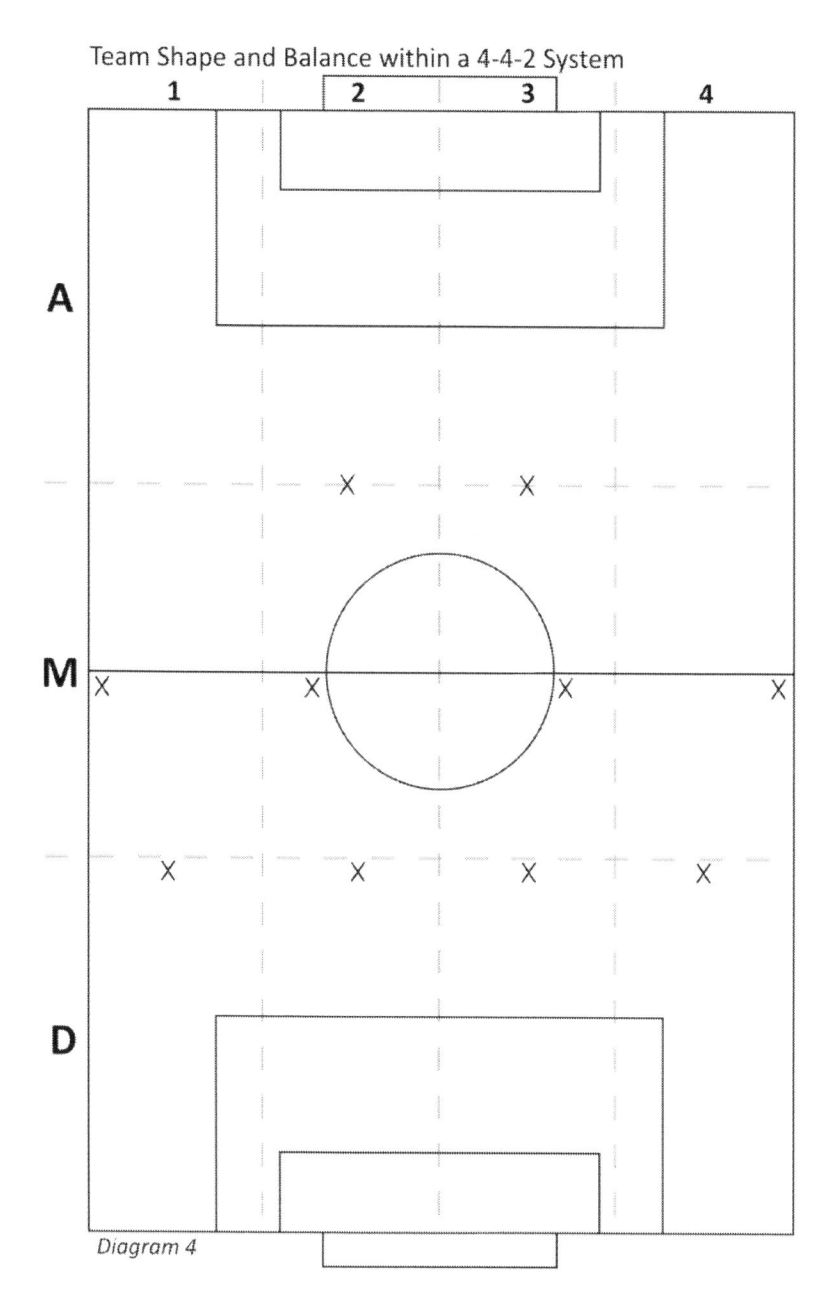

Team Shape and Balance within a 4-4-2 System

Diagram 4

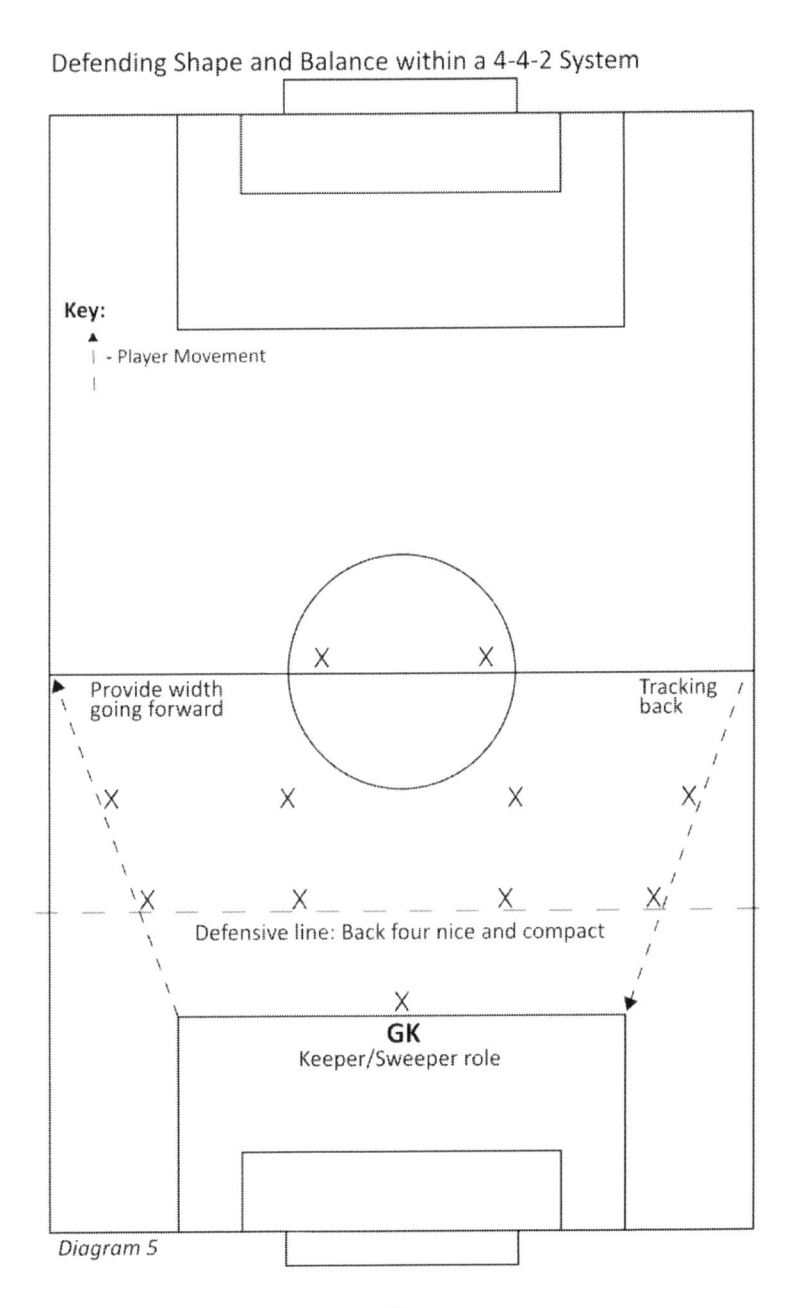

Defending Shape and Balance within a 4-4-2 System

Key:

▲
| - Player Movement
|

Provide width going forward

Tracking back

Defensive line: Back four nice and compact

GK
Keeper/Sweeper role

Diagram 5

A-Z FOOTBALL/SOCCER COACHING

Attacking Shape and Balance within a 4-4-2 System

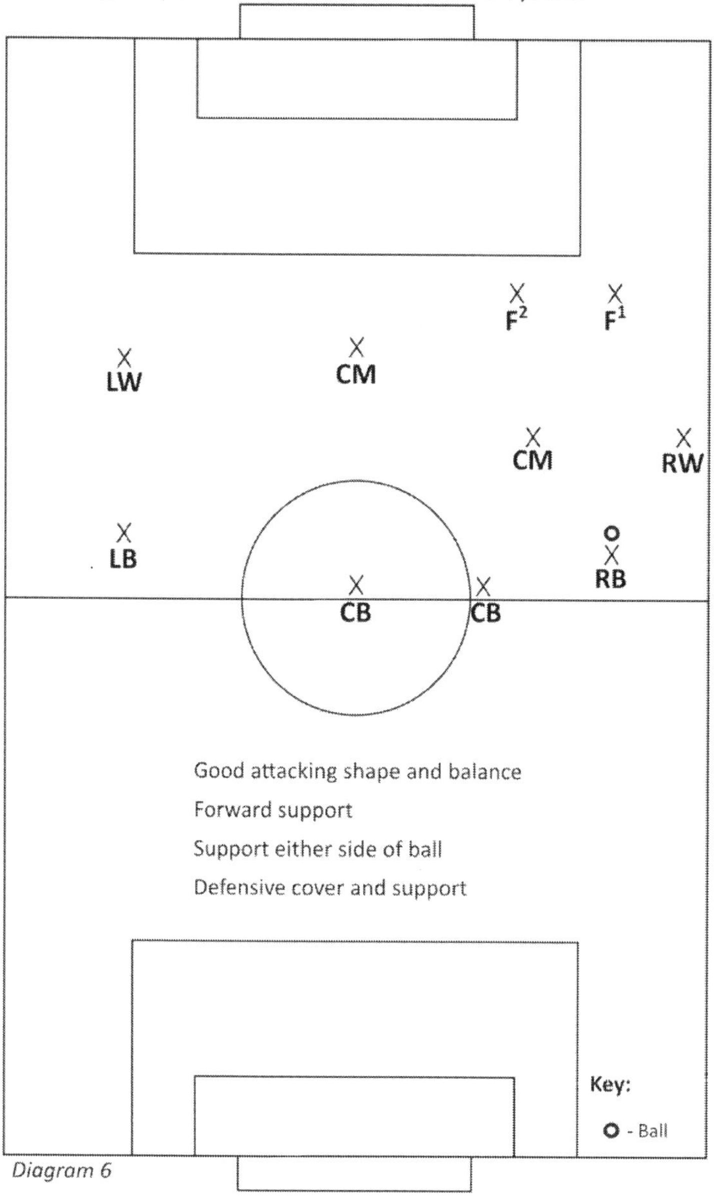

Good attacking shape and balance
Forward support
Support either side of ball
Defensive cover and support

Key:

O - Ball

Diagram 6

Principles of Football/Soccer

The principles of football/soccer can be divided into three basic categories depending on which type of play they effect.

DEFENDING – MIDFIELD – ATTACKING

Communication is vital to successful execution in all football/soccer situations.

DEFENDING *(Deny – Destroy – Develop)*

As soon as you lose possession.

MIDFIELD *(Build – Connect – Support)*

The link between defending and attacking.

ATTACKING *(Move – Receive – Finish)*

As soon as the team gains possession.

A-Z FOOTBALL/SOCCER COACHING

ATTACKING PRINCIPLES	*DEFENDING PRINCIPLES*
1. SUPPORT	*1. DELAY*
2. CREATION/UTILISATION OF SPACE	*2. DEPTH*
3. MOBILITY/WIDTH	*3. BALANCE*
4. ATTACKING BALANCE	*4. COMPACTNESS*
5. PENETRATION	*5. CONCENTRATION*
6. IMPROVISATION	*6. CONTROL/RESTRAINT*

WIDTH GOING FORWARD

COMPACTNESS WHEN DEFENDING

DEFENDING:

FIRST DEFENDER: A good starting position in relationship to your opponent and the ball will give you a better chance to be able to apply pressure. On your approach think, ' can I intercept, spoil or delay his forward movement. ' By looping your run and closing the space down quickly, you can dictate which way you want your opponent to go. Keep your eye on the ball, stay on your feet and be prepared to jockey him until such times you can make a solid tackle. Upon winning the ball you switch to attacking mode.

COVERING DEFENDER: The covering defender will take up his position off of the first defender. Good communication and distance are key to providing good cover. If the first defender has shown his opponent outside and he gets beat, the covering defender now becomes the first defender and applies the same principles while the first defender tries to offer support with his recovery run.

Away from the ball, the other defenders must provide good defensive shape and balance by also taking up good starting positions as well as marking and covering space.

When regaining possession of the ball and the ball is played forward, it is important to push up quickly together so as not to leave gaps.

When defending as a unit, I like my back four to hold a high line and to stay nice and compact to stop penetration. Concentration and communication is the key to a well organised defence.

MIDFIELD PLAY:

MIDFIELD: Often referred to as the engine room, it is the link between defending and attacking. Depending on what system you adapt will dictate the roles of your midfield players. When playing with three central midfielders, I am looking for a holding midfielder who will screen the back four, win tackles, organise and have a good range of passing. On either side of the holding midfielder, I am looking for a creative midfielder and an attacking midfielder. The qualities I am looking for in a creative midfielder are: the ability to play 360 degrees, a good first touch, comfortable in tight situations and has a good range of passing.

My attacking midfielder needs to be positive and forward thinking and prepared to run at the opposition. They should have a good first touch, link well with the front player's and kick in with 10 – 15 goals a season.

When playing as a unit, good angles and distance of support help keep good shape and balance. In a 4 – 4 – 2 the wide players stretch the opposition's defence when going forward. Good speed endurance, a change of pace and a good supply of crosses into our front players to attack is essential. It is also very important that the wide players also have a good understanding of the defending principles looking to tuck back in and to track back when the team loses possession.

FORWARDS: ATTACKING PLAY.

As I have already mentioned attacking play starts as soon as you regain possession of the ball so a positive mind set is a must. Movement asks questions of the opposition and good width going forward will stretch them defensively. Possession doesn't win games, but it gives you a better chance, so again, good support and creating space are key factors.

I am not a lover of just playing one up top because I think that player can get isolated. I much prefer a partnership or a unit of three. When attacking, I don't want my front players making runs into the wide channels and delivering the ball. I want my front players to look to get into the box at every opportunity and if we are playing with 3 we are looking to attack the near post, middle of the goal and far post areas. When playing with two front players, I am looking for the wide player on the opposite side to look to get in around the back. I also say to the wide player delivering the cross ' Make sure you miss out the first defender ' and to the strikers I say ' Remember the goal doesn't move so make sure you work the keeper.

Systems

When coaches talk about systems of play, I much prefer to think about team shape and balance, although I do think you need a foundation to play from. In choosing a system the coach must take into consideration such factors as:

1. Physical fitness of players
2. There ability to execute the basic techniques
3. There mastery of attacking and defending tactics

At the pro level, where teams have a scouting network, the game plan can change from game to game, depending on how the opposition sets up.

What ever system you play 3 – 4 – 3, 4 – 2 – 4, 4 – 3 – 3, 4 – 4 – 2 or a 3 – 5 – 2, it is about players knowing and understanding their roles. I don't care if I have two front players that between them, score 30 – 40 goals a season, they must understand they have defensive responsibilities as well. As I have mentioned a couple of times, the game is made up of defending and attacking principles and changes when a team loses or regains possession of the ball.

Good communication and discipline is key to the execution of how your team performs. Winning your individual battles, developing good partnerships and getting the units, defence, midfield and forwards working in cohesion, is what we strive for as coaches.

Plan B

I think it is important to have a Plan B. For example a team playing a 3 – 4 – 3 system could be vulnerable if the opposition play with 3 central midfielders and look to play balls into the wide channels in the defensive third of the pitch. In that situation I would probably go to a 3 – 5 – 2 and bring on a holding midfielder which would balance the overload in the centre of midfield and I would emphasise the importance of the three at the back slotting over and the two wide players looking to track back.

Patterns of play

Shadow play is a good way to teach how patterns of play develop all over the pitch. It also helps players to appreciate the types of passes to make, the positions to take up, the timing of runs to coincide with the passes (and crosses) in order to produce a successful attack. Shadow play can be used without opposition or with just 2 or 3 players applying pressure in different areas of the pitch.

Diagram 7 - Build up play in the defending half:

RB plays the ball into the front man who lays the ball off to the supporting CM. The CM plays the ball into the space for the RW to run onto it.

Diagram 8 - Build up play in the attacking half:

This time the RB plays the ball into the second striker who plays the ball around the corner between the two defenders for the first striker to run onto it.

Buildup Play in the Defending Half

RB Plays the ball into **F**

F Lays the ball off to **CM**

CM Plays a diagonal ball for the **RW** to run onto

Key:

○ - Ball

↑ - Ball Movement

↑ - Player Movement

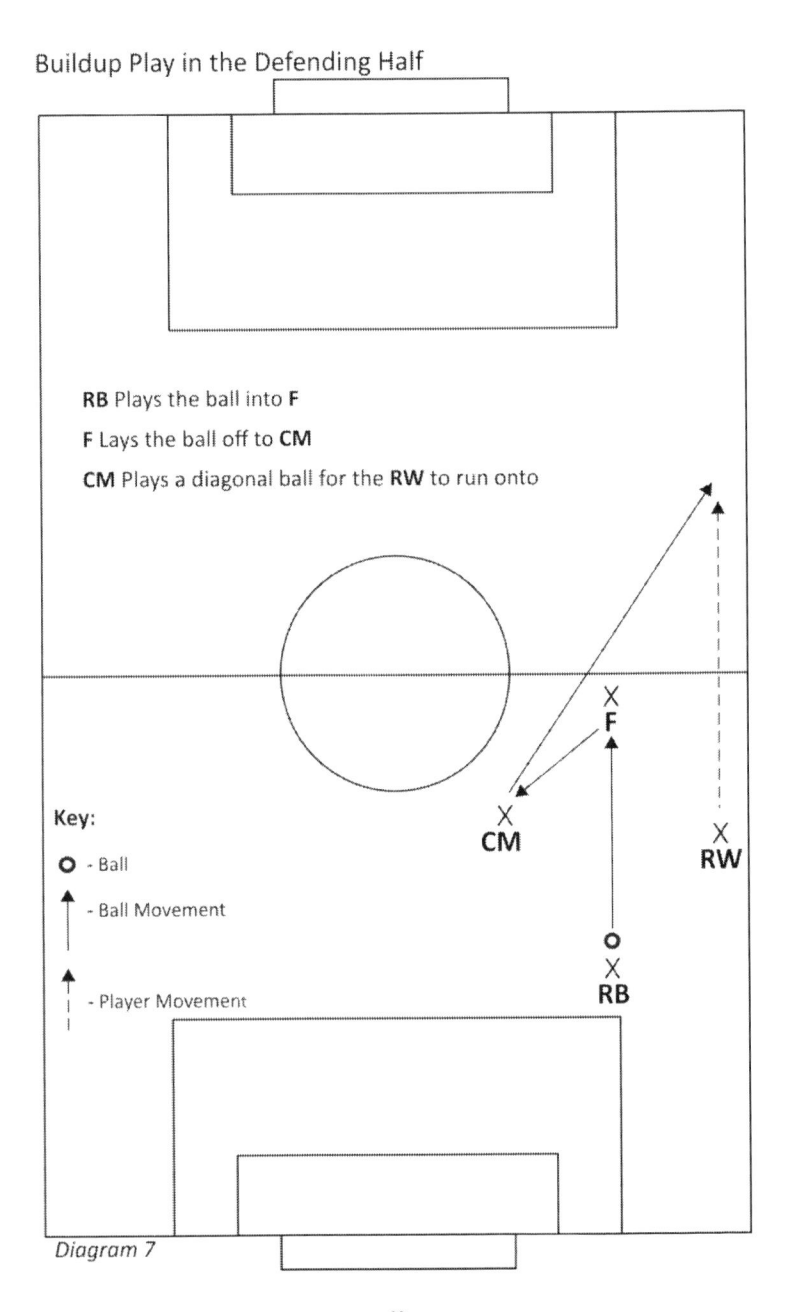

Diagram 7

A-Z FOOTBALL/SOCCER COACHING

Buildup Play - Attacking Half

Ball is played into **F²**

F² playes the ball around the corner for **F¹** to run onto

Route one to goal

Key:

○ - Ball

- Ball Movement

- Player Movement

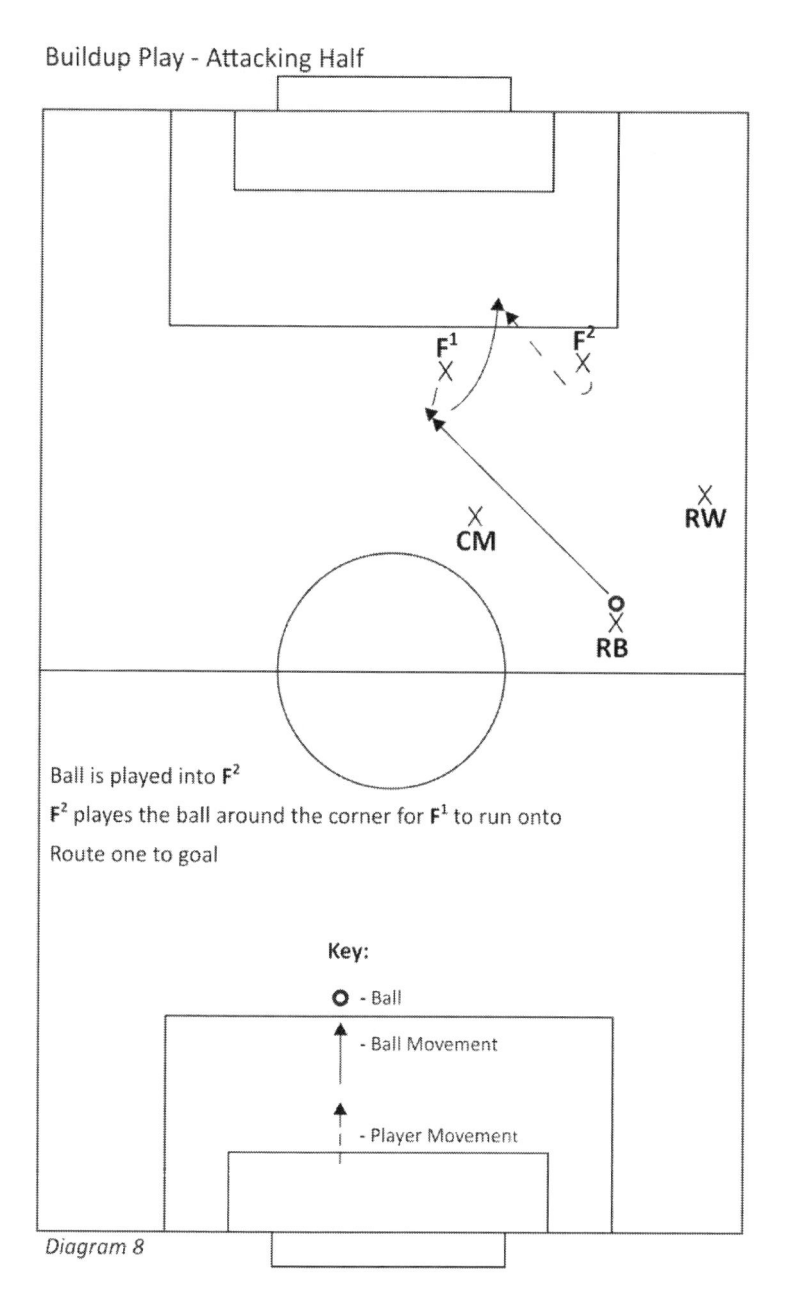

Diagram 8

8 v 8

When I went to Seattle to play we finished most of our training sessions with an 8 v 8 across half of the pitch using full size goals. Normally the shape of both teams would be 2 – 3 – 2 giving you two diamonds creating width and depth.

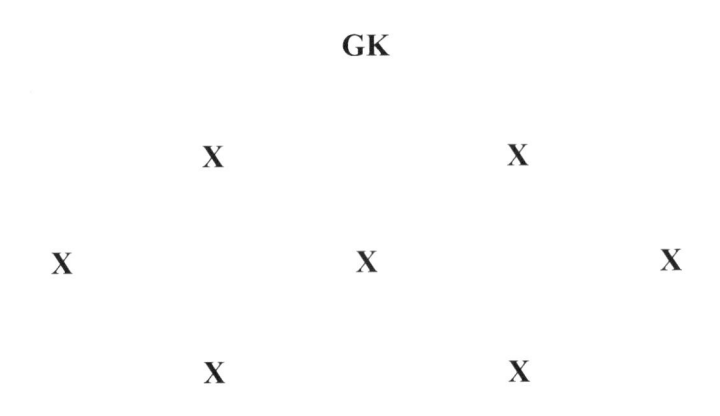

GK

X   X

X   X   X

X   X

The first team keeper and the reserve keeper would rotate so as to work with both the FBs and the CBs. Normally the starting 3 CM would play together with 2

Forwards up front. Not only did this get partnerships and units working together it created lots of 1 v 1 battles. When we needed to develop our wing play we would play from one penalty area to the other, disc's would be laid down the width of the penalty box creating a channel on either side for the wingers to work the channels and to get their crosses in. The FBs would also be added into the channel so as to work on support and overlapping runs.

Conditions would also added:

- Two touch – to move the ball quickly.
- No backward passes – to encourage passing and running the ball forward.
- Every player must be over the halfway line before your team can score a goal – to encourage your team to push up quickly together.

Set pieces

This is another part of the game I feel needs to be rehearsed regularly, defensively and offensively. Set pieces account for approx. 35% of goals scored in the game.

1. THROW INS
2. CORNERS (for and against)
3. FREE KICKS (for and against)

See diagrams 9a - 13

The key to good execution is to have the right players in the right areas and to have options.

One of my pet peeves is to give the ball away to easily at throw – ins. When we get a throw – in I am looking for two things:

1. To keep possession
2. To turn the opposition around

Signals, communication and movement triggers which option is going to be played.

Although we practice our set pieces in training I always post them on the board in the dressing room before the game. I do this for two reasons every one knows his role and if someone switches off I can point the finger.

Throw Ins

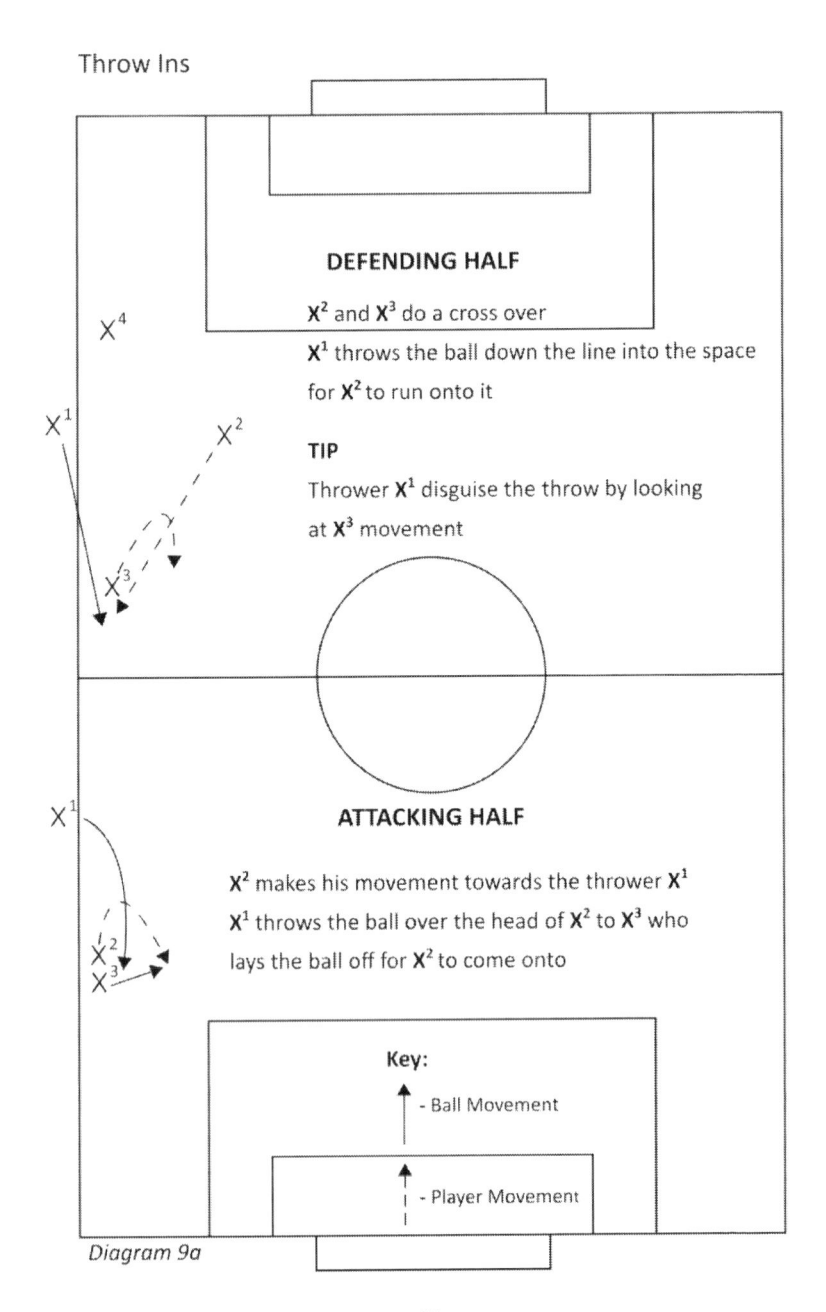

DEFENDING HALF

X^2 and X^3 do a cross over

X^1 throws the ball down the line into the space for X^2 to run onto it

TIP

Thrower X^1 disguise the throw by looking at X^3 movement

ATTACKING HALF

X^2 makes his movement towards the thrower X^1

X^1 throws the ball over the head of X^2 to X^3 who lays the ball off for X^2 to come onto

Key:

↑ - Ball Movement

↑ - Player Movement

Diagram 9a

A-Z FOOTBALL/SOCCER COACHING

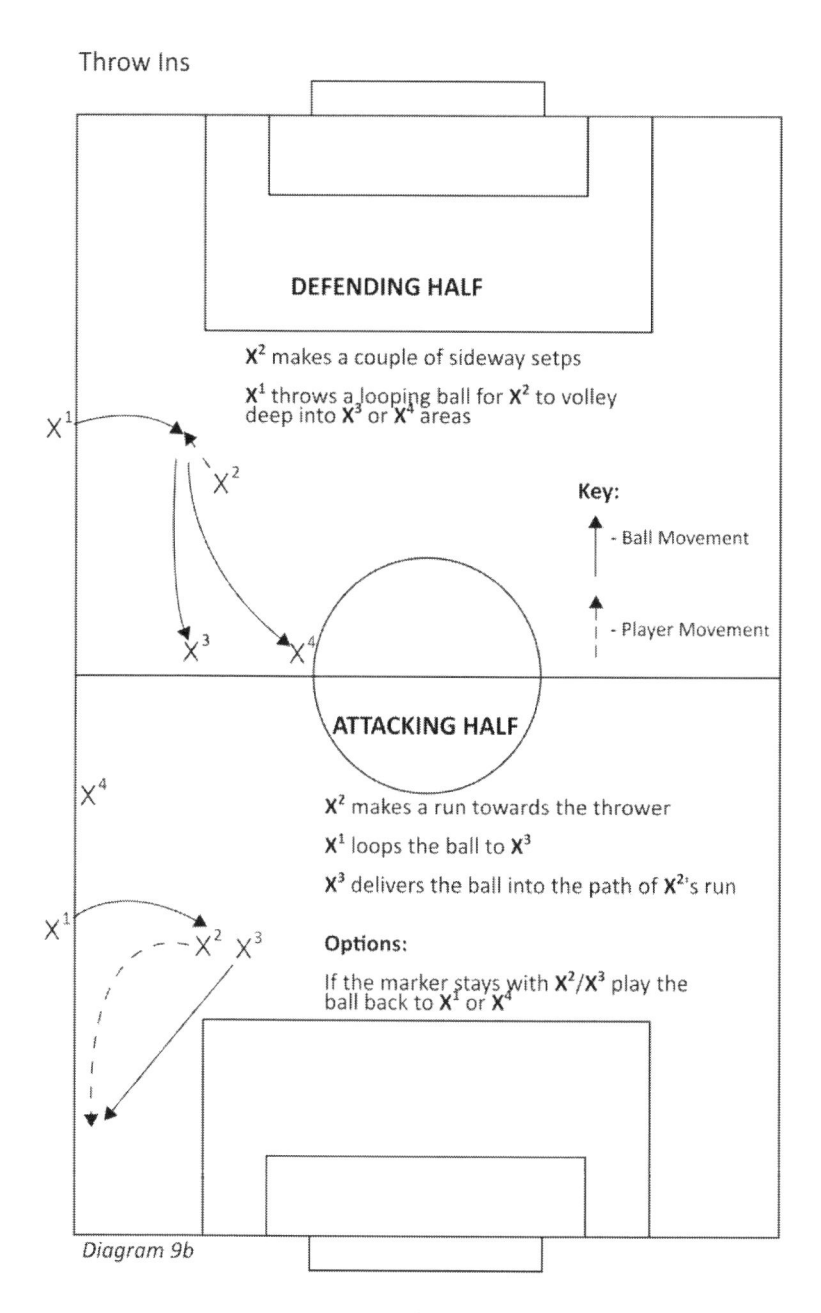

Throw Ins

DEFENDING HALF

X^2 makes a couple of sideway setps

X^1 throws a looping ball for X^2 to volley deep into X^3 or X^4 areas

Key:

- Ball Movement

- Player Movement

ATTACKING HALF

X^2 makes a run towards the thrower

X^1 loops the ball to X^3

X^3 delivers the ball into the path of X^2's run

Options:

If the marker stays with X^2/X^3 play the ball back to X^1 or X^4

Diagram 9b

Corner Against

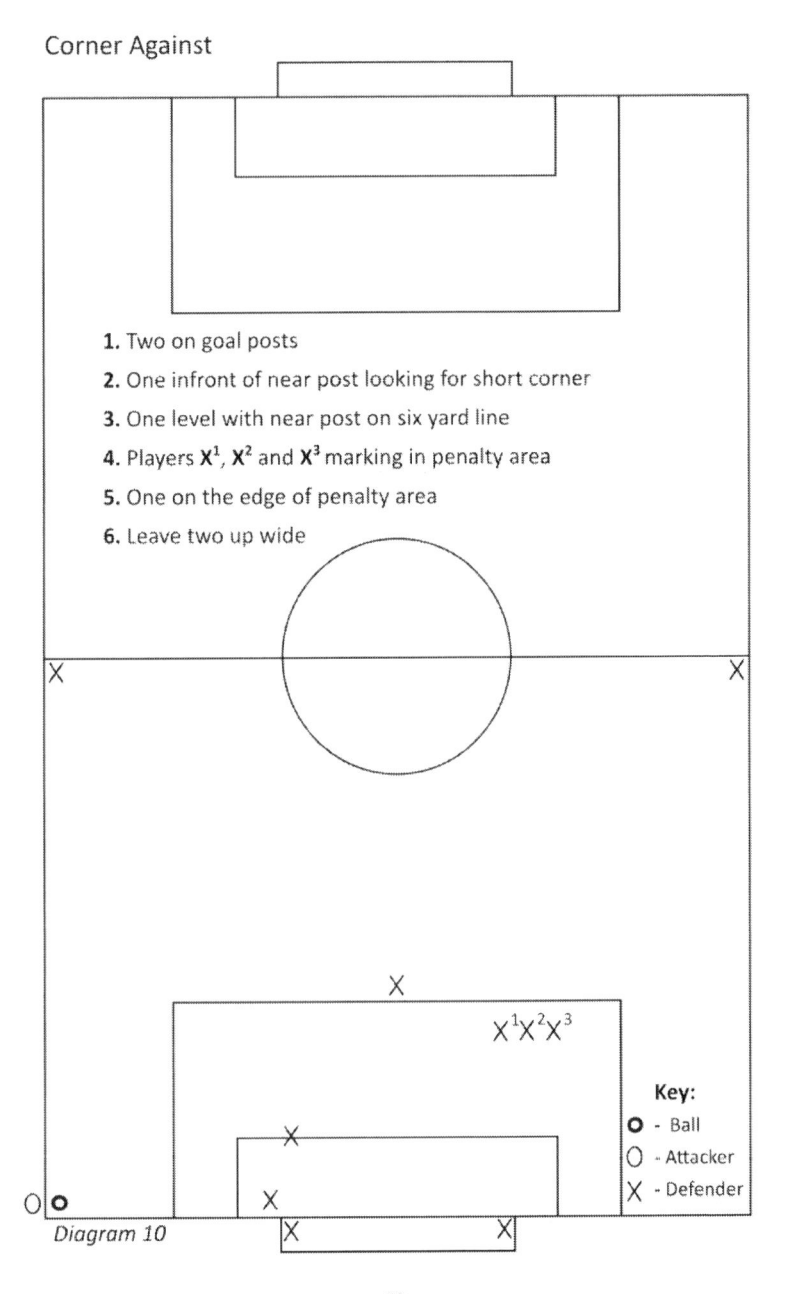

1. Two on goal posts
2. One infront of near post looking for short corner
3. One level with near post on six yard line
4. Players X^1, X^2 and X^3 marking in penalty area
5. One on the edge of penalty area
6. Leave two up wide

Diagram 10

Key:
- ◯ - Ball
- ○ - Attacker
- X - Defender

A-Z FOOTBALL/SOCCER COACHING

Corner For

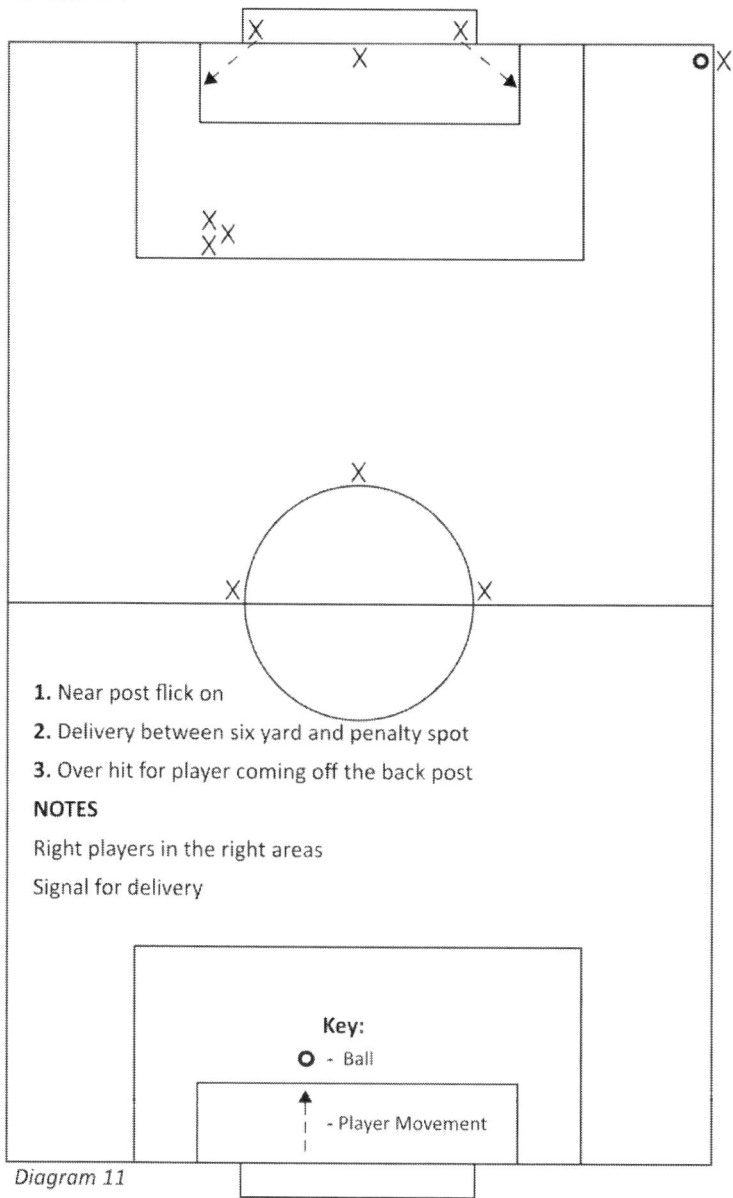

1. Near post flick on
2. Delivery between six yard and penalty spot
3. Over hit for player coming off the back post

NOTES

Right players in the right areas

Signal for delivery

Key:
- **O** - Ball
- ↑ - Player Movement

Diagram 11

Defending Freekick

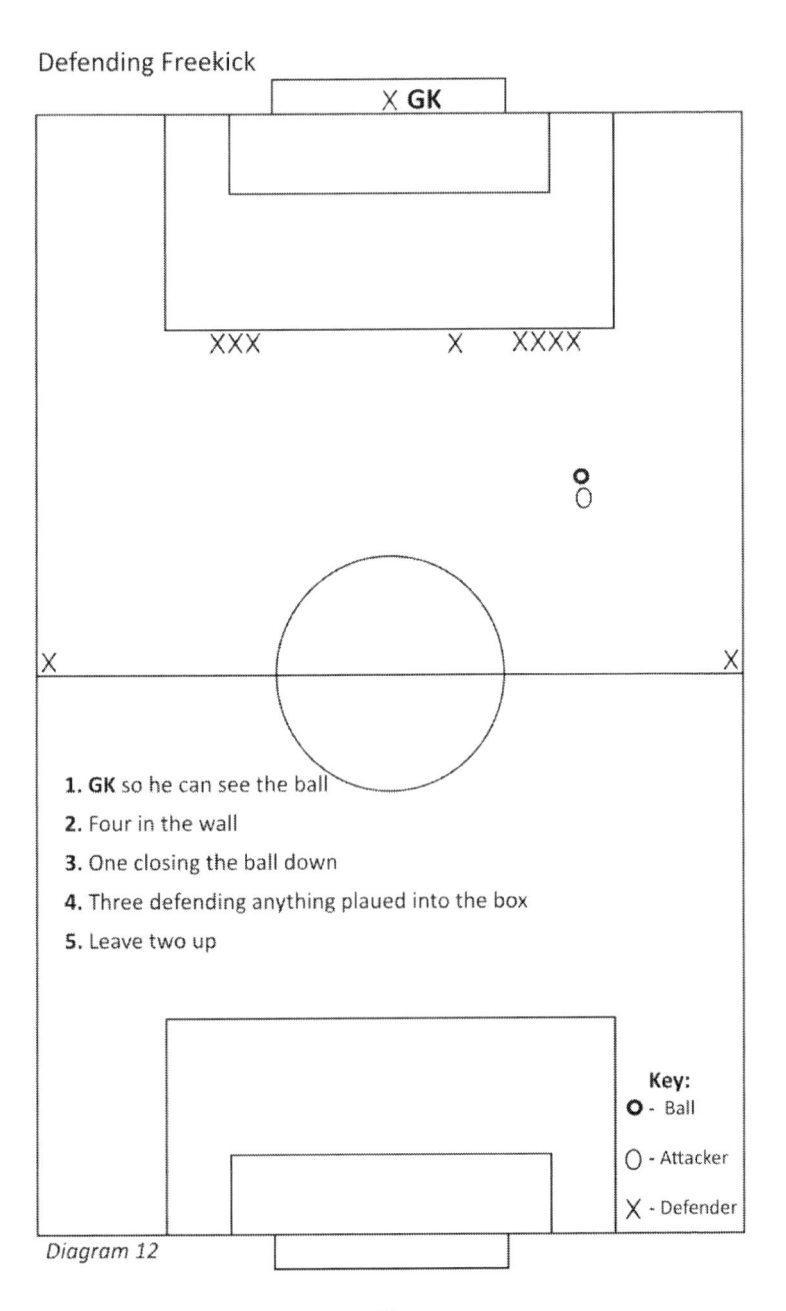

1. **GK** so he can see the ball
2. Four in the wall
3. One closing the ball down
4. Three defending anything plaued into the box
5. Leave two up

Key:
- **O** - Ball
- O - Attacker
- X - Defender

Diagram 12

A-Z FOOTBALL/SOCCER COACHING

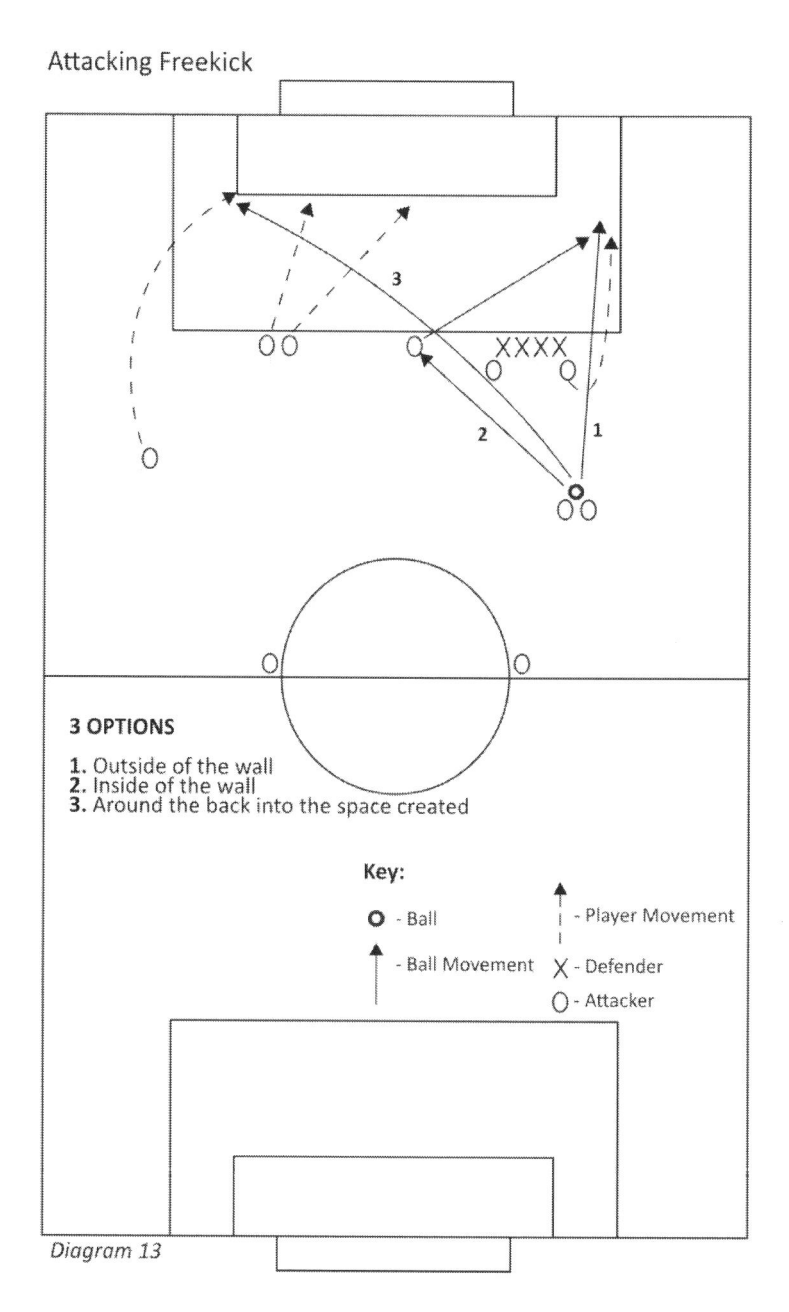

Attacking Freekick

3 OPTIONS

1. Outside of the wall
2. Inside of the wall
3. Around the back into the space created

Key:

O - Ball

– Ball Movement

– Player Movement

X - Defender

◯ - Attacker

Diagram 13

Components of Football/Soccer

1. **Technique**
2. **Tactics**
3. **Physical Fitness**
4. **Physiology (Mental Alertness)**

Technique: Coaching basic skills is based on a progressive pattern beginning with the fundamentals and leading to the more complex method of dealing with the ball.

EXAMPLE	Teaching passing technique
PROGRESSION	Fundamental – in twos
	Match related – 5 v 2
	Match condition – 5 v 5 two touch

Basic Skills:

1. Ball juggling (to develop a feel for the ball)
2. Passing
3. Shooting
4. Heading
5. Dribbling
6. Tackling
7. Control

Ball juggling: When I first got into coaching I was asked to warmup the group of players we were working with and as they all had a ball I got them to juggle it using the various body parts – feet, thighs and head. After about 5 minutes, the tutor came over and said to me " Do you see players in the game standing there juggling the ball ? " I replied ' No ' He then said, " So make it more game specific and get the players moving with the ball. " I thought straightaway that makes sense, however I do think juggling the ball is a good exercise to help improve your touch and balance and gets you using both sides of your body.

Passing: All players, especially from an early age, should be encouraged to use both feet.

What is the most important ingredient in a good pass, accuracy or the weight of the pass?

The **weight** of the pass is the most important because even if you are slightly off with your pass, if the weight is right the receiver can always get to it.

Basically there are three types of passes:

1. Push pass, played with the inside of the foot over a short distance.
2. Driven pass, using the lace area of your boot and is played with pace
3. Chip or lofted pass, using the big toe area of your boot when you want to get the ball up and over an obstruction.

When making a pass the decision is whether to play the ball into feet or space.

Shooting: While coaching the U16 Youth Academy at Colchester United, I attended a coaching clinic in Newcastle – Upon – Tyne, in the north of England. One of the topics on the course was shooting and one of the senior coaches put on a shooting session. He started by selecting ten coaches who were all ex pros. He asked them to hit a half volley from about twenty yards out, trying to beat the GK by aiming for the corners of the goal. One or two found the corners, but most hit the ball wide of the goal. He then asked them to try to hit the GK on the knees with the ball. Again one or two hit the target but this time most of the shots went into the corners of the goal.

With young players, I tell them to make sure they work the keeper and to follow up on all shots. Players have to remember the goal doesn't move, so when having to take a touch first, try to set the ball to give yourself a good angle to get a quick shot off. If at a slight angle from the goal and you are looking to get a shot off hit it hard and high at the GK. When in a wider position hit it hard and low across the GK.

Heading: With defensive heading, you are looking for height and distance. Therefore, keep the head steady and head the ball slightly below centre using the forehead. A lot of players struggle because they expect the ball to drop perfectly onto their head. Read the flight of the ball, work your feet and jump towards the ball.

When I was an apprentice at Colchester United, the trainer, Denis Mochan, would have a bag of balls in the centre circle. We would start inside the penalty area and he would hit balls into the air for us to come onto and head clear. We did this a couple of times a week, heading between 10 – 20 balls per session.

Attacking Heading: This time you are looking to guide the ball down to a teammate, or beat the GK when in an attacking position on goal. Therefore, we want to head the ball slightly above centre. For this exercise Denis would serve the ball from the goal post, changing posts after 10 headers. We would start our run from the edge of the penalty area and meet the ball between the penalty spot and the six yard box. He would then progress it by getting the wingers to cross balls in for us. We were taught that when the winger puts his head down to cross the ball to make your first movement away from the ball and then come back onto it. We would work on glancing the ball towards the near post or looking to head the ball back in the direction the keeper had come from.

Dribbling: When I think about players dribbling the ball the player that comes to mind is George Best. George had tremendous balance and was very brave which can be seen on a lot of footage of him playing for Manchester United. He had great close control, the ability to beat his opponent either side with a change of pace and direction. He was very positive in his play and it can be measured by the number of goals he scored and the assists he had. There are a lot of players that are good at running and dribbling with the ball but have no end product. Not only did George score and set up goals, he won a lot of corners and free kicks and at the end of a dazzling run, he usually forced the keeper into making an incredible save. The key to making it difficult for your opponent is to keep the ball moving.

Tackling: At times I think defenders feel that they have to try to win every ball, when the first thing they should do, is to make sure they are goal side and ball side of the player they are marking. The best time to make the tackle is when your opponent is just on the half turn and you can see the ball better.

Block Tackle: In a 50/50 challenge for the ball, lower your centre of gravity, stay on your feet and when making the tackle get your full weight behind it.

Slide Tackle: Defenders are encouraged not to go to ground but to stay on their feet. Usually a slide tackle is more of a desperation tackle where you are stretching for the ball. The best place to make a slide tackle is close to the touch line where you are less likely to get caught out.

Control: There are two ways of bringing the ball under control:

1. Cushion control
2. Wedge control

Cushion Control: Try to get your body in line with the ball. Select the surface you intend to use foot, thigh, chest or head. On contact relax the body part ie, if using the head bend through your legs. Ideally you want to control the ball into the space slightly in front of you.

Wedge Control: Again get in line behind the ball and by placing your foot or chest over the ball you stop it from bouncing backup at you.

When controlling the ball, your first touch is important. Think ' control and manoeuvre ' which will give you a little bit more space and time. If your first touch is forward, be positive and look to run or pass the ball forward.

How to Setup: I think the key to a productive session is to utilise the time you have available with the players. Below is the structure I learned at my FA Coaching License (UEFA ' B 'Award) I attended when I first returned from the States.

1. Introduce topic
2. Organise
3. Demonstrate
4. Sufficient practice
5. Correct problems
6. Summarise
7. Next stage

Tactics

What are tactics?

1. Tactics come into play when there is opposition.
2. Competing for ball possession.
3. Recognition of options and making decisions.

Progression:

Individual Tactics	1 v 1				
Group Tactics	2 v 1	2 v 2	2 v 3		
	3 v 1	3 v 3	4 v 2	4 v 3	4 v 4
	5 v 4	5 v 5			
Team Tactics	6 v 4 through 11 v 11				

Individual Tactics: To improve and develop a player's ability to handle the 1 v 1 situation that is common in football/soccer.

Group Tactics: Learning what to do as a group around the ball is the objective of group tactics.

Team Tactics: In teaching team tactics, the coach must concentrate on both the individual performance and combination play. He must mould a unit of up to 11 players that will have the capacity of both defending and attacking.

The use of restriction is a valuable method of teaching team tactical play.

Coaching Grid: The grid is usually marked off in either a square or rectangular shape and is used to work on a tactical problem.

Physical Fitness

Physical fitness training involves exposing the body to higher levels of work than it is accustomed to.

The Integral components of physical conditioning are:

1. Endurance
2. Strength
3. Flexibility
4. Speed
5. Coordination
6. Agility

Endurance: Sustaining an effort without undue fatigue over a period of time.

Strength: Maximal force or power of which muscles are capable.

Flexibility: The range of motion possible at a joint.

Speed: The ability to move from one point to another in the least possible time.

Coordination: To perform a skill as efficiently as possible without wasting body movement.

Agility: The ability to move with quickness and ease. (Change direction with and without ball).

Methods of Training

Interval training: Short work bouts interspersed with rest periods.

Circuit training: Continuous work involving different muscle groups.

Fartlek: Continuous running while changing speeds.

Pressure training: Another form of interval training. Technique under pressure of time and fatigue.

Economical training: Training sessions that combine at least two of the four basic components of football/soccer.

Functional training: Is specialised in the particular skills necessary for playing a specific position. Training under game conditions that stresses a player's technical or tactical weakness.

The three running exercises in Diagrams 14a and 14b are variations of many different exercises I did as a player and used as a coach.

Doing the Star Run with the ball gets the players working at getting the ball out from under their feet as well as taking their mind off of the run and without the ball helps their endurance.

Speed endurance: Is important when you make a forward run, it breaks down and you have to get back quickly.

Game specific: Incorporates the different types of runs you make in a game, forward, backwards and sideways.

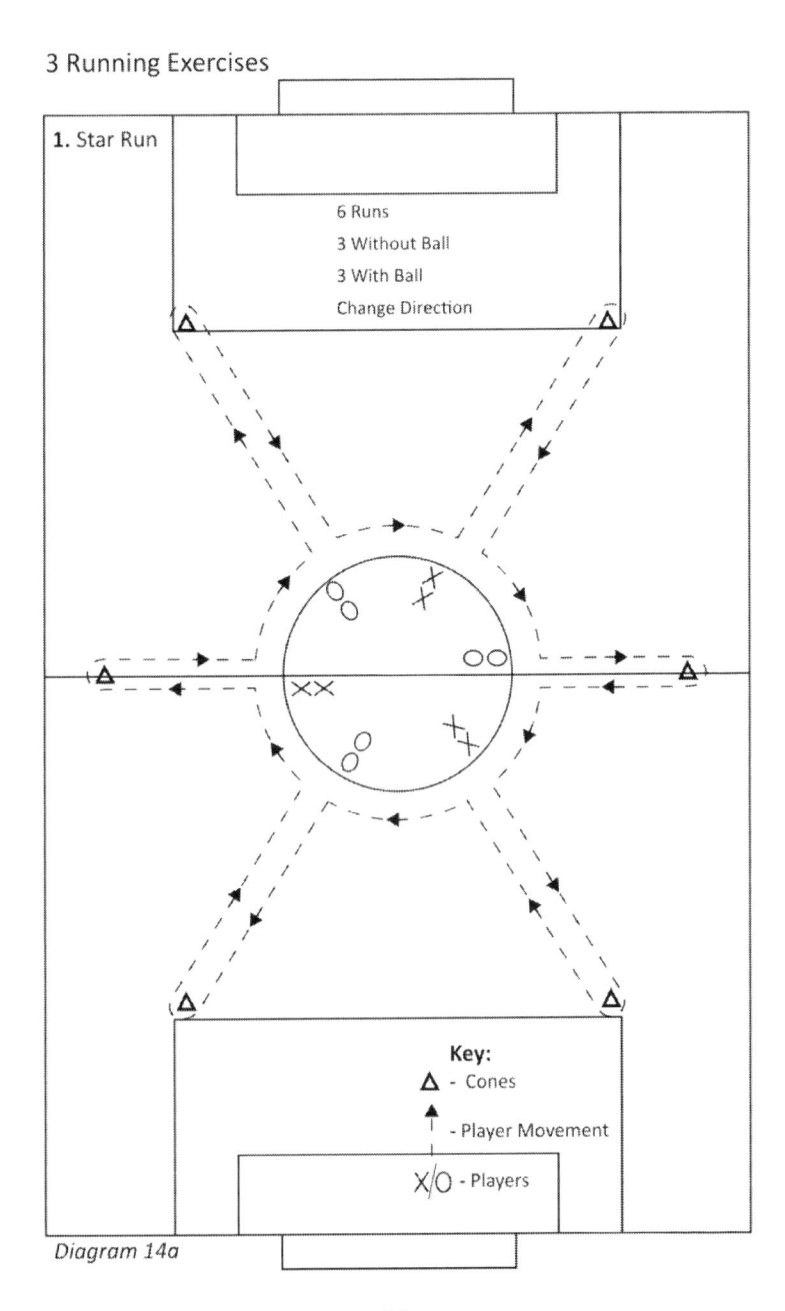

3 Running Exercises

1. Star Run

6 Runs
3 Without Ball
3 With Ball
Change Direction

Key:
△ - Cones
↑ - Player Movement
X/O - Players

Diagram 14a

A-Z FOOTBALL/SOCCER COACHING

3 Running Exercises

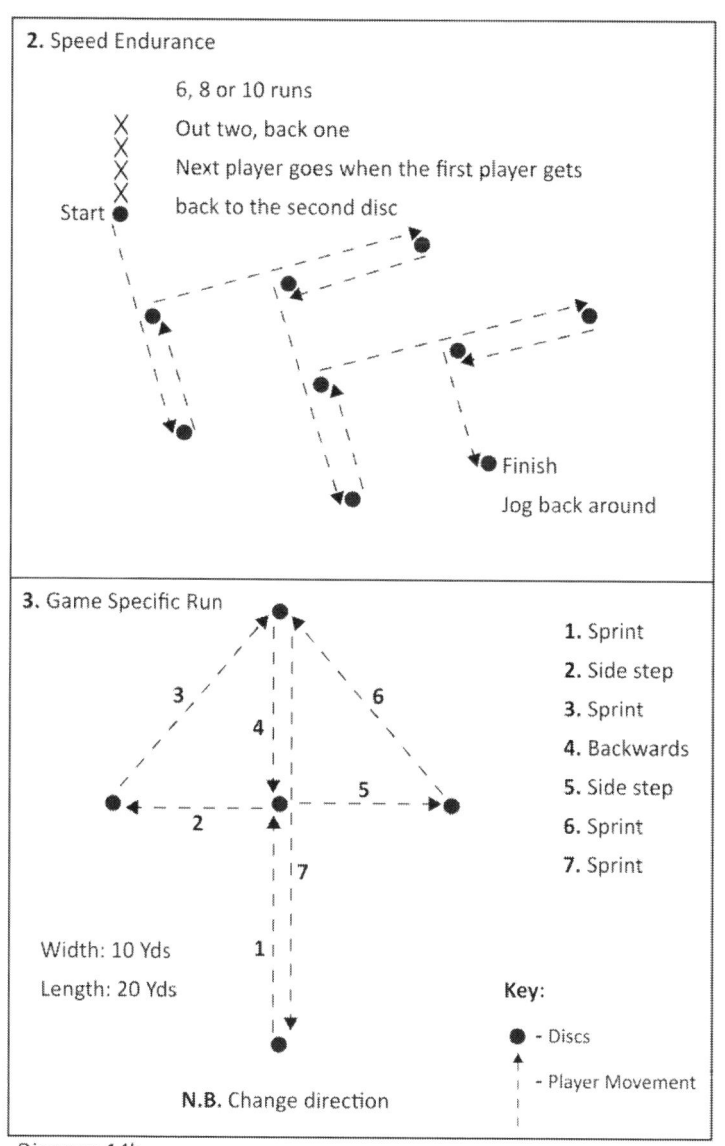

2. Speed Endurance

6, 8 or 10 runs

Out two, back one

Next player goes when the first player gets back to the second disc

Start

Finish

Jog back around

3. Game Specific Run

1. Sprint
2. Side step
3. Sprint
4. Backwards
5. Side step
6. Sprint
7. Sprint

Width: 10 Yds

Length: 20 Yds

Key:

● - Discs

↑ - Player Movement

N.B. Change direction

Diagram 14b

Psychology – Mental Alertness

As coaches, we want to try to get the best out of our players.

We must remember that when working with youth players, they are all striving to develop their own identity, so how we deal with one individual may not be the right approach for another. This is an interesting part of the game and can be very frustrating.

As players get tired, they begin to make mistakes. This is when the psychological dimension is tested; who has the mental toughness to battle on even when making mistakes and to continue to run, work and talk.

Coach Best in his pre – match talk, would always say it was about winning your individual battle and that if he had seven players winning their battles, we always had a chance of winning the game, knowing on the day one or two might have an off day.

Today, there are lots of debates about the pressure put on young players to win. My personal feeling is that up to the age of twelve (going into their teens), the emphasis should be on technical development. I do believe that a player's development is ongoing, and I do not see anything wrong in trying to develop a winning mentality. Even today when I am playing games with my grandchildren, I play to try to win. As you move up the ladder as a player, coach or manager, winning games is how you are judged, and I think you should use losing a game as an incentive to do better and work harder.

Principles of Coaching

Key factors in coaching:

1. Purpose (Topic)
2. Objectives
3. Priority order and logical sequence
4. Planning and organisation
5. Observation
6. Communication - by showing, demonstrations and verbal

The qualities of a good coach:

1. Enthusiasm
2. Integrity
3. Persistence
4. Patience
5. Good standards
6. An open and enquiring mind
7. A logical and analytical mind – the ability to diagnose

8. Knowledge of how players learn
9. Knowledge of the principles of effective coaching
10. The ability to inspire

Teaching: Individual and team meetings, be consistent with your philosophy.

The Coach – Player Relationship

In watching the performance of a couple of Premier League managers/coaches, I feel the relationship between the player and the coach is very important to the success of the team. My observation in looking at Mourinho and Klopp is that the biggest difference is that the players at Liverpool want to play for Klopp, whereas when Mourinho was at Manchester United, it was obvious there was a lack of respect.

Players need recognition as they proceed to develop their own physical stamina, skills and tactical ability as a member of a team. The coach not only teaches, evaluates and physically prepares his players he must be able to motivate them to fulfil their potential.

Coaching Youth

1. The coach not only teaches the game he must take into consideration the players mental and physical development. Beginning at the age of six and up to fourteen, is a time for learning

football/soccer. The coach should base his plans on the maturity, strength, fitness and attention span of the players.

2. Ages 6 – 8: The emphasis should be on having fun.

3. Ages 8 – 10: Introduce basic techniques. The emphasis should be on increasing enjoyment through improving play.

4. Ages 10 – 12: Introduce all techniques and team play with more intense exercises.

5. Ages 12 – 14: Work more intensively on the techniques introduced at the 10 – 12 year level.

6. Ages 14 – 16:

    a. Basic skills must be perfected.
    b. Able to apply all the skills under pressure of opponent and with restrictions of time and space.
    c. Knowledge of principles of play and team tactics is required.
    d. A heavier physical fitness training schedule to improve endurance and strength

7. Age 16 – 18: Players should perform at close to their maximum potential. There techniques must be polished under game conditions and there tactical training should be completed.

Coaching without playing experience

This is not a handicap, a playing background is not a necessity. A key to being a successful (and I don't mean winning) youth football/soccer coach, is to draw upon your experience. If you grew up playing sports of any kind, you possess some knowledge of good and bad coaching techniques.

DON' T

1. Become frustrated
2. Yell and intimidate
3. Be afraid to adjust your training activities if the children are not enjoying them.

DO

1. Keep players active with a ball
2. Vary the activities based upon attention span
3. Enjoy yourself
4. Be positive to all players, not just the stars

If your are going to put some time into the development of young players, you should also look at putting some time into developing yourself.

The following are some suggestions on how we can go about it:

1. Attend coaching clinics
2. Read football/soccer books
3. Watch higher levels of play
4. Ask and take advice of experienced coaches in your area

FINAL NOTE: As coaches we sometimes have a tendency to take the decision – making away from the players. Remember, the best teacher is the game itself.

Leave the coaching until your next practice session.

Organisation

A well organised session can be accomplished in 1 ½ hours

6 – 10 years old   1 hour

11 – 16 years old   1 ½ hours

SESSION:

1. Technique (ball each)
2. Tactics (topic)
3. Conditioned game (incorporate topic)

EQUIPMENT: An adequate playing surface

YOURS

THEIRS

1. Cones/Markers

1. Ball (for teaching)

2. Bibs

2. Shin pads

3. Stopwatch

3. Boots/Trainers

4. Balls/Pump

4. Appropriate clothing

Stretching should be done as a warmup before training and a warm down after training.

Pre – Season

My last season 2018 – 19 I helped Tom Austin with the pre – season over at FC Clacton a senior men's team. Our pre – season was over a six week period that included friendly games that started on the third weekend.

Training was on Tuesday and Thursday evenings, from 7:30 pm to 9:00 pm and Saturday mornings 10:30 am to Noon, working with a squad of sixteen players.

Obviously depending on who you are coaching and the numbers available will determine the intensity of your sessions.

Week 1.

Warm up - Different movement patterns – stretching.

Tuesday – 12 min. run.

Thursday – 12 min. run.

Saturday – 12 min. run.

Ball work – individual and in pairs. (Comfortable with the ball)

8 v 8 (free play)

Cool down.

Week 2.

Warm up.

Tuesday – 3 groups on a running track 8 x 220 yards run (¾ pace)

Thursday – 3 groups on a running track 10 x 220 yards run (¾ pace)

Saturday – 3 groups on a running track 8 x 220 yards run (sprint)

Technical Work – feet, thighs, chest and head.

8 v 8 Conditioned game (two touch)

Cool down.

Week 3.

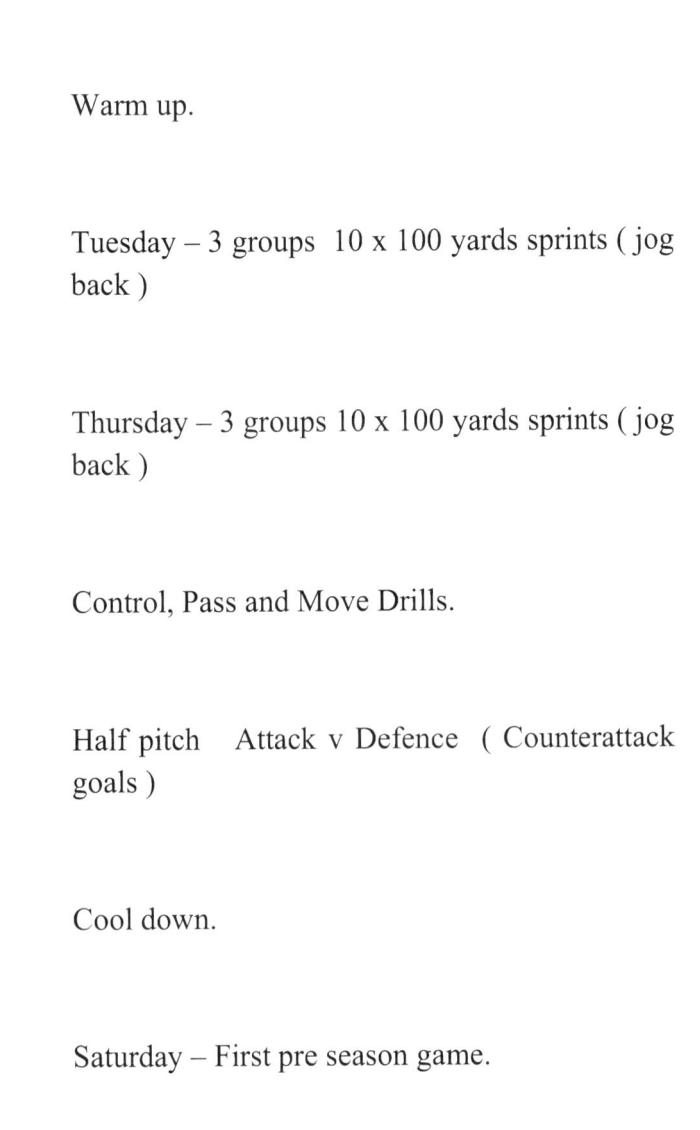

Warm up.

Tuesday – 3 groups 10 x 100 yards sprints (jog back)

Thursday – 3 groups 10 x 100 yards sprints (jog back)

Control, Pass and Move Drills.

Half pitch   Attack v Defence   (Counterattack goals)

Cool down.

Saturday – First pre season game.

Week 4.

Warm up.

Tuesday – 2 groups 10 x 30 yards sprints (jog back)

Thursday – 2 groups 10 x 30 yards sprints (jog back)

Finishing.

Shadow Play looking at the mechanics of playing 4 – 3 – 3 (Shape and Balance)

Cool down.

Saturday – Game.

Week 5.

Warm up.

Running with the ball (change of pace and direction)

Crossing and Finishing.

Set pieces (for and against)

8 v 8 Full pitch (width of penalty boxes)

10 x 10 yards Explosive sprints.

Cool down.

Saturday – Game.

Week 6.

Warm up.

Tuesday – 2 groups 10 x 10 yards sprints.

Thursday – 2 groups 10. 10 yards sprints.

12 v 4 Keep ball 1 Touch 2 Touch 20 x 30 yards grid 2 mins.

Finishing.

Set pieces.

Cool down.

Saturday – Last pre season game.

If we had been working five days a week like the pros, our running pattern would be as follows:

Week 1. Twelve minute run on a grass track looking for the players to improve the number of laps daily.

Week 2. Three groups two hundred and twenty yard runs 6 8 10 8 6 Increase/Decrease by the end of the week the players are flying.

Week 3. Two groups one hundred yard sprints, jog back 8 10 12 10 8 Again by the end of the week players are looking sharp.

Week 4. Thirty yard sprints 8 10 12 10 8 Explosive!

Conditioned games

Once pre season is done and we are into the regular season I like to play a lot of keep ball sessions and conditioned games. In the keep ball sessions I like to vary the number of players and use different size and shaped grids. I also like to play 1 and 2 touch, to encourage moving the ball quickly.

See diagram 15

With the conditioned games we predominantly play 8 v 8 normally on a 60 x 40 pitch using the full size goals. It is a great way to have a theme for your session based on a particular segment of the game you feel you need to work on.

See diagrams 16a and 16b

Various Keep Ball Sessions

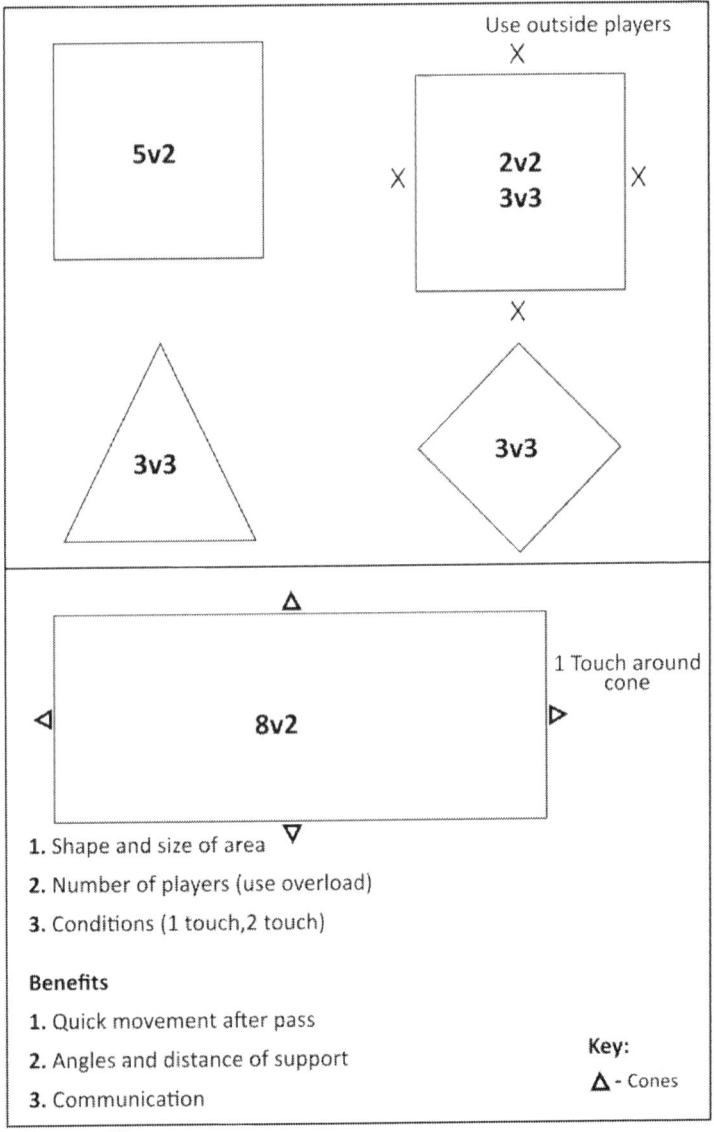

5v2

Use outside players
X

X 2v2
3v3 X

X

3v3

3v3

△

◁ 8v2 ▷ 1 Touch around cone

▽

1. Shape and size of area
2. Number of players (use overload)
3. Conditions (1 touch, 2 touch)

Benefits

1. Quick movement after pass
2. Angles and distance of support
3. Communication

Key:
△ - Cones

Diagram 15

A-Z FOOTBALL/SOCCER COACHING

Conditioned Games

1.

40yd / 60yd box with X at each corner, 6v6 2MF inside

6v6 Keep ball session

2 **MF** players play on team in possession

X returns the ball to team in posession

Movement - Awareness

Recieving - Turning with the ball

Passing - Pass selection

Variation switch play:

X crosses to opposite **X** to play the ball back in

2.

Key:

X/O - Players

⛳ - Goal Posts

Half Pitch

6v6, GK between goal posts, O and X at corners

7 metre goal

6v6

4 Corner players

Use corner players to rotate with

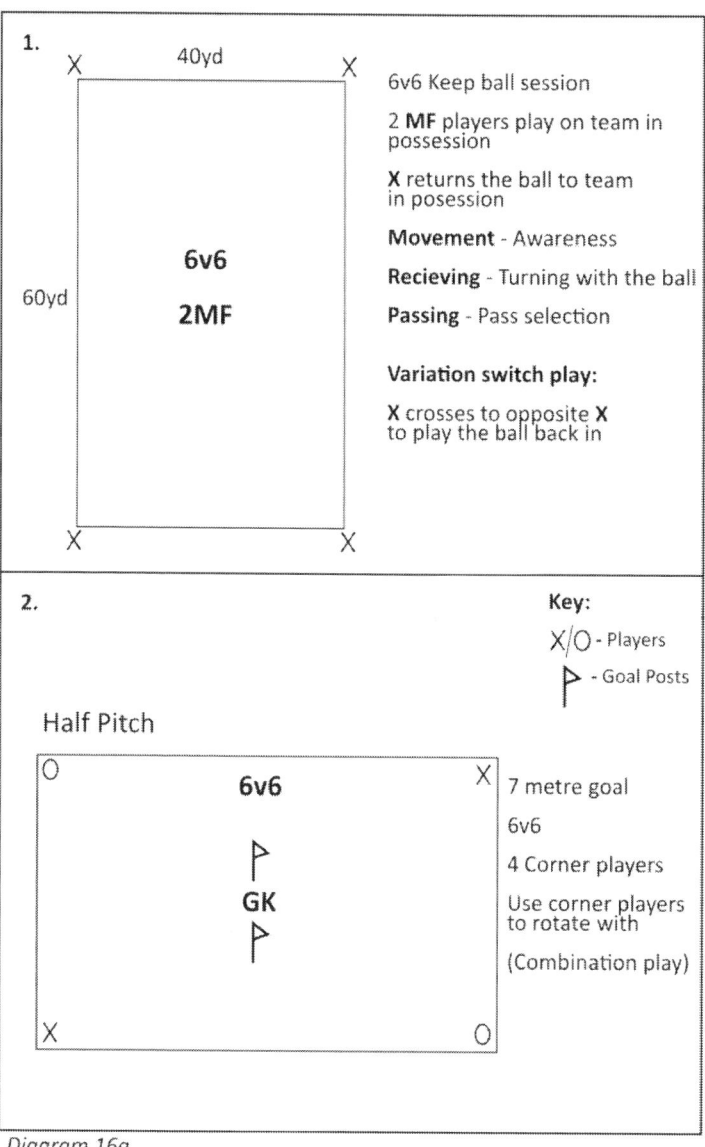

(Combination play)

Diagram 16a

Conditioned Games

3.

4v4

- Diamond shape
- Attacking principles
- Defending principles
- Free play

Field: 25yds × 35yds, with 6yds marked

KS — positioned top
X, X — middle sides
X — bottom

Key:
KS - Keeper/Sweeper
O - Ball

4.

8v8

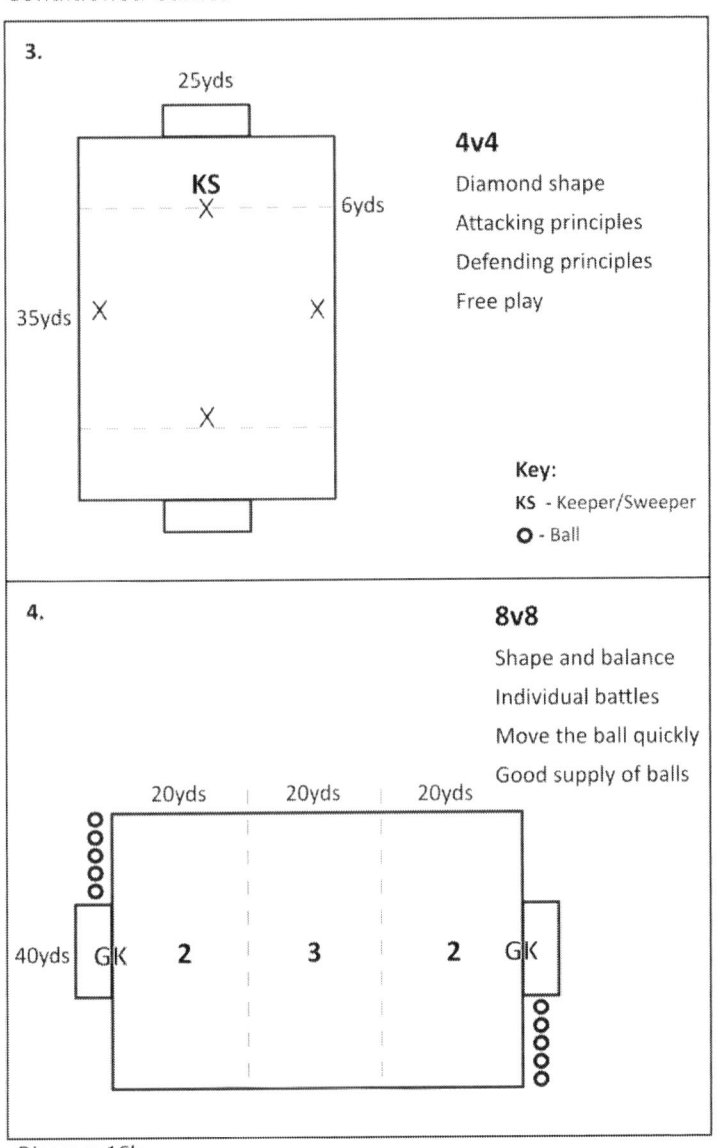

- Shape and balance
- Individual battles
- Move the ball quickly
- Good supply of balls

Field: 40yds wide, divided into 20yds | 20yds | 20yds sections
GK — 2 — 3 — 2 — GK

Diagram 16b

Role Models

Looking back over the years I would have to say early doors there were two coaches that influenced and encouraged my love for the game. The first was Peter Hurst the PE teacher at my secondary school. A former pro player himself he had a tremendous work ethic, every night after school he would be there for me and my school mates and in the five years under him we only lost one game. The other was John Chandler who was also a PE teacher at one of our rival schools. John also ran the Youth team for Colchester United and at fourteen he took me under his wing. At fifteen I made my debut for the Youth team and at fifteen and a half I played half a dozen games for the reserves in the London Midweek League, playing with many of the first team players.

I think the next stage of my football/soccer development was when I went to play for the Seattle Sounders in the NASL 1974 – 79. During my time there I was very fortunate to play under four great coaches –

Best, Gabriel, Howe and Redknapp. All four had very good playing careers and individually and collectively were also top coaches.

John Best did not perhaps have the playing career in England that the others had but that did not stop him from being a very good coach. It was obvious that he was a student of the game and was meticulous in getting across in training how he wanted his team to play. He would always finish his team talk before a game by saying if we want success today, we must have 7 players winning there individual battles. This is something that has stuck with me and I always remind my players knowing on the day there will be one or two that might have an off day.

Jimmy Gabriel not only had a great career playing for Everton, Southampton and Scotland he was without doubt the best coach I played under. Not only did he lead by example, he would also talk to you about what he thought your weaknesses were and spend time on the training field showing you the right way. His demonstrations were superb (a picture paints a thousand words).

When he became Head Coach, he moved me back into midfield and made me team captain. This was a great honour for me and I would have run through a brick wall for him. He knew how to get the best out of his players and this showed in our playoff performances and in the 77 Soccer Bowl Final.

I didn't really get to see a lot of Bobby Howe as a player but knew he played for WestHam in the days of Moore, Hurst and Peters. Jimmy had played with Bobby at Bournemouth and when he took over from John Best he made Bobby his number two. In fact Bobby had to play the first couple of games of the 77 season while we waited on players coming over.

What I learned from Bobby is that you could do a two hour session in an hour and a half if you are well organised, done your homework and let the session flow rather than keep stop/starting it. His attention to detail was top drawer and I think his success as a coach with the Sounders can be measured by the fact that he worked under Gabriel, Hinton and Calloway.

Finally there was Harry Redknapp, who started his career with WestHam and like Bobby Howe played alongside the 3 World Cup Winners Moore, Hurst and Peters. Before joining the Sounders in 76 he played with both Jimmy and Bobby at Bournemouth. The three had always said that if the opportunity came up they would like to work together.

When Jimmy took over as Head Coach he decided he wanted to have a reserve team, a place for the young American players to develop and that became Harry's role. What I loved most about Harry's style of coaching was that there was always an element of fun involved and everything revolved around working with the ball. Harry did a great job of preparing these young players to make that step up to the first team and under his guidance, players like Jimmy MacAlister, Jeff Stock, Mark Peterson, Bernie James, Eddie Krueger and Ian Bridge all went on to have successful careers.

It came as no surprise to me that when Harry returned to England he went on to have a very successful managers career in the Premier League.

My Football/Soccer Philosophy

1. A good fitness base.

2. Understanding of defending and attacking principles.

3. Players comfortable with the ball.

4. Good team shape and balance.

5. Control, pass and move.

6. Angles and distance of support.

7. Good range of passing.

8. Forward thinking.

9. Communication

10. Decision making

Summary

If when I left school in 1968 to join my home town club Colchester United as an apprentice someone had said to me I would go on to have a career in football/soccer spanning 50 years I would probably have fallen over laughing. To be honest I feel very privileged to have been involved as a player, coach and manager for so long. I have been to some fabulous places and played with and against some of the all time greats of the game.

When I first went over to North America I could not believe the facilities and some of the stadiums we played in were just incredible. Today I think the Premier League has taken football to another level. Recently I visited my favourite team Tottenhams new ground. What a facility!

Shortly after I returned to England I got back involved at my hometown club, Colchester United where I worked for 13 years in youth development. A few years into working at the club the whole structure throughout the country changed as funding was made available to set up Academy programs for kids U9 – U16, which also opened the door for lots of coaches to get involved.

Over the years, there have been many changes in and around football/soccer, the game loved by so many all over the world.

Some of the changes to the actual game since I was an apprentice are the number of subs (when I first started playing it was one), the back pass to the keeper (he can not pick it up now), the offside rule (which is still causing problems) and certainly the introduction of the foreign players into the league. Although it has been great for the fans to see so many of their favourite players playing, I think it has been somewhat detrimental to the development of our young players.

The manager merry – go – round still continues and for whatever the reasons, we are not seeing as many ex players going into coaching.

After having surgery on my back in October 2019, and in between doing my rehab, I found myself watching a lot of Premier League game's (before the Coronavirus Pandemic) and to be quite honest, I found them to be a bit boring. What I mean by that is, a lot of the teams are trying to adapt the Man. City style of play (playing out from the back), and in my opinion, they are not good enough. For me, there are too many backward and square passes that are being intercepted and teams are getting punished. On paper, Wolves and Sheffield

United don't have the strength and quality of some of the top teams, however what they have brought to the league is a good work ethic and a bit more directness in their play.

This got me thinking about what these teams are doing in training and how has modern day coaching changed the game. When I was a player, I was taught when receiving the ball to try and have an early picture, get the ball out from under your feet and look to play it forward. By doing so you straight away asked questions of the opposition.

I don't want to be seen as advocating the long ball game, because for me, it is more about getting the balance right. (Decision making). In today's modern game we do have great players in Messi and Ronaldo but in the games I have been watching I don't see to many players that can pick a pass or a George Best type player that will run at defenders with the ball, or a David Beckham who could deliver a pinpoint cross.

The exposure that football/soccer gets worldwide through TV and media coverage, is enormous. In my day, it was Saturday night "Match of the Day" and the FA Cup Final.

I think there will always be comparisons made between now and then but I will always say George Best would still have been the player he was today, playing in these wonderful stadiums on carpet like pitches.

Ever since I can remember I have always been a Tottenham fan (not a lover of Mourinho) however I do like the way Man. City play under Pep Guardiola the movement of the ball is a joy to watch. If not the best coach in the world he must be right up there. Another coach I admire is Jurgen Klopp for his coaching knowledge and particularly how all of his players want to play for him.

I think football/soccer has certainly been highlighted during the lockdown due to the Coronavirus and just how much we have missed it. I think it just shows what a big part the game plays in the lives of so many people.

Fantasy Football

When Adrian Webster finished playing at a professional level he started his coaching journey. It was his dream to one day coach the Seattle Sounders or a Premier League club. After spending 50 years involved in the 'Beautiful Game' he thought about what he had learned and to share his knowledge. If he was to become Manager/Coach, what would he teach his young players from his vast experience of having played and coached at many levels of the game?

With coaching diagrams, drills, and a general insight, this book can be passed on. Whether you coach at the pro level or are just coaching a young player, Adrian's book covers in-depth basics for all levels of players.

A Guide to Soccer and Coaching Ade's Way

Adrian Webster wants his coaching book to be different. This book shares his views and experiences of having been involved in the game as a player, coach and manager at youth, college and pro levels. He started to get involved in coaching when he first joined the Seattle Sounders in 1974. Because you have played the game, doesn't necessarily make you a good coach, this was another thing he took on- board from his first coach, John Best. You need to become more aware of how we learn and that coaching is very much like teaching. Adrian believes that good verbal communication and visual demonstrations became his focus and as they say, a picture paints a thousand words.

Circle of Life: A Life, A Career, A Passion from Former Seattle Sounders Team Captain

A professional soccer career that spans 50 years. Follow Adrian Webster on his Soccer Journey that took him from his home in Colchester to Vancouver BC, Seattle, Pittsburgh, Phoenix and finally back home to where he's retired.

Playing for the Seattle Sounders 74 – 79 in the NASL, he played against his two idols Pele and George Best. In 1977 Head Coach Jimmy Gabriel made him the team captain and that season he lead the team to the Soccer Bowl Final in Portland. In 2017 Adrian returned to Seattle, home of the MLS Champions where he was awarded the Golden Scarf for his contribution to Soccer in the Great Northwest. Come along and enjoy Adrian's journey of ups and downs.

A man who played alongside the legends of soccer.

Adrian Webster

Adrian Webster played for the Seattle Sounders NASL '74-'79. As a young lad growing up in England, his favourite players were Pele and George Best.

In 1977, Head Coach Jimmy Gabriel made him team captain and that season he lead his team to the Soccer Bowl Final in Portland. On the way to the final, he was voted Man of the Match for his man-marking performance on George Best and in the final he came up against his other idol, Pele.

During his six seasons with the Sounders, he played with and against some of the greats of that era.

Books to Go Now

You can find more stories such as this at www.bookstogonow.com

If you enjoy this Books to Go Now story please leave a review for the author on a review site which you purchased the eBook. Thanks!

We pride ourselves with representing great stories at low prices. We want to take you into the digital age offering a market that will allow you to grow along with us in our journey through the new frontier of digital publishing.
Some of our favorite award-winning authors have now joined us. We welcome readers and writers into our community.

We want to make sure that as a reader you are supplied with never-ending great stories. As a company, Books to Go Now, wants its readers and writers supplied with positive experience and encouragement so they will return again and again.

We want to hear from you. Our readers and writers are the cornerstone of our company. If there is something you would like to say or a genre that you would like to see, please email us at inquiry@bookstogonow.com

Printed in Great Britain
by Amazon